The Disciple's
School of
Prayer

By Brendan Case

www.BrendanCase.com

A City of the Lord Publication

Phoenix · Los Angeles · San Diego · Monterey Bay

Publisher: City of the Lord
711 W University Drive
Tempe, Arizona 85281
480-968-5895
www.cityofthelord.org
PhoenixBranch@cityofthelord.org

City of the Lord is officially established as a Private Association of the Christian Faithful and Private Juridic Person of Diocesan Right by Bishop Thomas J. Omsted, May 8, 2012. City of the Lord is also a founding member of the Catholic Fraternity, a private association of the Catholic faithful, established in the Vatican by Pope Saint John Paul II on November 30, 1990.

Printed in the United States of America.

The Disciple's School of Prayer
Written by Brendan Case
Cover art by Brendan Case

ISBN - 13-978-0-9915327-3-5

Acknowledgements

Jesus, gratitude fills my heart as I sit to thank those on whose shoulders I have stood to write *The Disciple's School of Prayer*. Jenelle Van Brunt and Bonnie Tyminski have been so kind to clean up my destructive use of the English language and Jim Hyde always makes me look good by editing the layout and artwork for my books. You, my sisters and brother, have sacrificed for the Kingdom and I pray that the Lord Jesus richly reward your children and your children's children with an abiding love for Jesus in his Church. Thank you Jenelle, Bonnie and Jim.

Father, thank you for my girlfriend who happens to be my wife, Andrea. You, Andrea, my love, stand with me before the Father, waiting to fulfill his will and trusting his providence, *living "All for the Gospel!"*. You remind me often that you loved me first and for this my heart swells. You, also, along with the Father, are my *Relentless Pursuer*. You consistently reveal to me the loving ways of the Blessed Trinity. Thank you!

Lastly, I am grateful to my Constant, Abiding, Companion, the Holy Spirit. You, my Friend, take and use me, a broken vessel with whom you are in love, and pour your gifts through me so that I may glorify the Father. I sit at this keyboard and the words spill out of my fingers effortlessly. This means, to you be the glory for *The Disciple's School of Prayer*. I pray it will reach many souls and set them ablaze so that you, Spirit of my *AhDah*, might renew the face of the earth. Let your Kingdom come!

More, Jesus, more!

With all the love in my heart, I am your little brother in Jesus,

Brendan, son of the Father

Table of Contents

Day 1: Enrolling in The School of Prayer

"Lord, teach us to pray..." Luke 11:1

MEDITATION

As was my habit, it was 6am and I arrived at my favorite coffee shop, Java City. It was there that I went to enter into my time of Lectio Divina, an ancient way of meditating on the Word of God, as I sipped on my Arnold Palmer and enjoyed my toasted, poppy seed bagel, smothered in cream cheese. I had convinced myself that this was the secret, hidden method of the mystics throughout the centuries. Before me was my Bible, my journal and my pen. Person upon person would fly in and out, getting their coffee on the run, and person upon person would ask, "What's the good word for the day, Brother?"

My prayer was always simple, "Speak, Lord, your servant is listening."

That morning I opened my Bible, ready to enter into weeks of studying from Luke 11, the Lord's Prayer. Over the years I had read many a book about this foundational prayer of the Christian faith. I knew that I would at least fill one of my 250-page journals, which was now blank, for the coming insights that I would receive.

My eyes read the familiar passage:

One day, Jesus was praying in a certain place. When he finished, one of his disciples said to him, "Lord, teach us to pray, just as John taught his disciples."

It was as if I could go no further. The Spirit of God had something to teach me in those few words, and I was not to proceed. My mind tried to move into the words of the Our Father, but it was back to that request that my spirit returned. Back and forth, I tried and tried to move on.

My bagel was consumed and the appointments for the day were placing their demand. I ended with the Our Father, the one I hoped to study, closed my Bible and journal, loading them into my back pack. I left Java City, but I did not leave that humble request of the disciples. My mind moved on, yet my heart was focused.

The day progressed and the request of the disciples keep mulling through my spirit. As I was focused on something else, suddenly, the direction was clear. I was to enroll myself in Jesus' *School of Prayer*.

"Lord, teach me to pray."

Given I was the youth minister, I had the keys to the kingdom at the parish. My adoration time was 2am on Friday morning. The chapel was right off the school. At 1:45am I would arrive and go to the school and borrow from it what every student needs. Into the chapel I would walk, carrying a desk I had borrowed to place it before the monstrance. I would take out my textbook and notebook, which was my Bible and journal. Out came my pen, I laid it on the desk, folded my hands, looked at Jesus in the monstrance and said, "Jesus, I am here for your *School of Prayer*. Lord, teach me to pray."

For months, this was how I spent my time with our Eucharistic Lord. During those quiet hours in the middle of the night I learned lessons regarding prayer that stay with me to this day, lessons by which I live.

If you are reading this book you have probably been blessed from childhood to this day by others who have shared with you, prayers and methods of how to pray. You have probably tried ways you have created. You might be with the few who have said,

"Jesus, teach me to pray."

If you have not laid before Jesus this entreaty of few words, today is the day you are invited to do so. Today is your day to enter the *Disciple's School of Prayer*.

Does it not seem wise that at least once in our life to say, from our heart, this short prayer, inviting Jesus himself to become our instructor, meditating on his words concerning the great art of prayer? How he must long for souls to make this modest appeal that is the key to all within the Kingdom of God.

I find it interesting that the Savior of the world sent forth his apostles to preach his good news, yet he gave them no formation as to how to preach; he gave them no outlines of truths to lay upon souls. One thing after another is given to the believer to accomplish for the greater glory of God: marriage, family life, just business dealings. Yet, no instruction, no schooling is provided. The reason is simple. The *School of Prayer* will provide all that we need for all that we live.

O believer, take no more time to consider. The time is now. Enroll yourself in the *Disciple's School of Prayer*.

PRAYER

Jesus,
I am ready.
I want to learn from you how to pray.
I realize that learning to pray is one of the greatest lessons your Spirit has to offer me.
Holy Spirit,
Jesus said you would lead me to all truth.
Teach me to pray.
Jesus,
it is my will and desire to enter into your School of Prayer.
Father,
thank you for this opportunity.
In Jesus' name.

ACTION

- Purchase a journal which you will consecrate and use for the Disciple's School of Prayer. Make sure to have a Bible, your journal, and a pen ready for the daily lesson in the School of Prayer.
- With whom and what will you share from today's lesson?

REFLECTION QUESTIONS

Who would you say are the people who have most helped you in your life of prayer?

What ways of prayer have been most helpful to you?

What would you like Jesus to teach you in the *Disciple's School of Prayer*?

What questions or concerns do you have as you enter into *The Disciple's School of* Prayer?

When and where is your best place and time to enter into prayer?

FURTHER READING

Matthew 4:18-22

Matthew 9:9

2 Chronicles 7:14

Mark 8:34-38

Day 2: Prayer is Being With

Pray then like this: "Our Father in heaven..."
Matthew 6:9

MEDITATION

When I first came to Jesus, Sister Gerard gave me one book after another about the faith. As time passed I found myself drawn to the ones on the spiritual life, Ascetical Theology. By the time I was seventeen years old, I had ravenously consumed many of the works of Saint Teresa of Avila, Saint Therese of Lisieux, all the works of Saint Louis de Monfort, much of Thomas Merton, along with Adolphe Tanquerey's *The Spiritual Life.*

I would add to my list the works of Saint John of the Cross, but the truth be told, when I read Saint John, it went in one eye and out the other. I also read countless books on teaching the ways of different devotions. Later, I was blessed to be introduced to Father George Maloney, Bishop Kalistos Ware, and the *Way of the Pilgrim*, inviting me to what I had never imagined.

My shelves were filled with books regarding Benedictine spirituality by authors such as Esther DeWalh. **The *Ladder of Divine Ascent* by** Saint John Clamicus was yearly reading for Lent. Then there were the books of Charismatic spirituality which encompassed both Catholic and Protestant authors. In the end, these books left me worn out, worried that I might not really know how to pray. It was not their fault. I was just immature.

Let me stop and say that the way of prayer is so simple that a child can enter its doors and find himself lost in the presence of God, while the aged practitioner can spend years plumbing His depths. Do not worry about where you are in the spiritual life. Grow from where you are, being who you are, at the moment. Let the Saints pull you forward, but do not compare yourself to them. A mystic is not a special type of person; each person is a special type of mystic.

Until I entered Jesus' *School of Prayer*, around the age of 30, I was in a quandary. How was I to pray? Was I missing something? Why was I not better at prayer, given I had been seriously pursuing it since I was sixteen years old? The answer was not complex. I was missing the most important aspect of prayer and it was the first lesson I learned in the *School of Prayer,* which Jesus tailored for me.

Sitting at my desk in the Adoration Chapel, hands folded with Bible and journal open, in the dark of the new day, a whisper came to my heart. What it said brought great peace and the anxieties which I faced about the spiritual life melted away.

"Brendan, prayer is not what you do. It is who you are with."

The point of prayer is not so much to do something as it is to be with Someone. I had been so caught up in the methods and the approaches that I missed the Person who rushed into my presence when I turned my heart in His direction. What He was looking for was to be with me and I had all these tasks to accomplish. No doubt that there are things to be done during prayer, but if we miss the Person who is first wanting us, then we miss the greatest blessing of prayer. Prayer is, first, about a Father who wants to be with His children.

This changed everything. Now I began my prayer by stopping and recognizing the One before me. For me, this stopping to recognize the Presence became a tuning of my heart to being loved and standing in the mystery of something greater than me. I must admit that because of turning my heart and recognizing the Presence, many times my prayer goes no further than being with Him and all that I wanted to accomplish is laid before Him in trust. At other times, what I needed to do goes far beyond what I could have done within myself. At other times, it is an act of trust because there is no experience, no awareness, yet I know that He has been with me, though I might not sense being with Him.

The principle of stopping to recognize the presence of God can also become a way of life for the Disciple. In the 17th century, Brother Lawrence wrote what is now a Christian classic, **The Practice of the Presence of God**. Brother Lawrence became a Carmelite Friar with a great longing to spend his life in prayer, but instead he was assigned to the kitchen where he could hear the other brothers chanting the Liturgy of Hours. Yet, the Spirit of God stirred in the forgotten brother's heart and taught him to do all things in the presence of God and with God. In this way of prayer, one does not add more prayers to his life. One lives his daily life and recognizes the presence of God in whatever he is doing and he chooses to be with Him.

One day I was going out to feed our chicken when suddenly I sensed the presence of the Holy Spirit walking beside me. With the 50-pound bag of feed on my shoulder, I halted. The Sprit of God said to me,

"What are you doing?
"I am feeding the chickens," I replied with a dumbfounded tone in my voice.
"Can I feed the chickens with you?" he asked.
Now, even more flabbergasted I inquired, *"You want to feed the chickens?"*
"No, I just want to be with you."

I know this might sound cutesy, but there is a profound truth which emerged in that moment. O, Disciple, do you hear it?

PRAYER

Father,
I want to be with you.
But what is more amazing is that you,
the All Powerful, the Creator of All that Is, the Immeasurable One,
want to be with me.
Please forgive me for all the times I have come to prayer and without having been with you.
Holy Spirit,
teach me to pray in Jesus' *School of Prayer.*
Give me the grace to stop and be with you.
In Jesus, name.

ACTION

- Today, just sit in His presence. Set aside your devotions and plans. Simply be with Him. Close your eyes and let the Holy Spirit use your sanctified imagination to reveal that he is with you. Let him be the Lord of the Encounter.
- With whom and what will you share from today's lesson?

REFLECTION QUESTIONS

Before reading this lesson, what would you have said as being the first movement of prayer?

What difference do you think it would make in your prayer time if you first stopped and recognized the presence of God?

Have you ever *practiced the presence of God?* Why not give it a try and see what happens?

FURTHER READING

Psalm 139

Psalm 42:2

Psalm 63:1

Psalm 143:6

John 7:37

Isaiah 55:1

Day 3: Jesus is Praying for You

"I ask not only on behalf of these, but also on behalf of those who will believe in me through their word..." John 17:20

MEDITATION

My son, Sean, had his friends Gene and Billy over to play. Sean had just turned 13 years old a few days before. The boys, along with my son, Tim, had just got out of the pool and were running down the hall to go into Sean's room to play video games. To me, this was a great time to share with him, in the sight of his friends, the amazing news I had received from a recent phone call.

"Hey, guys, check this out!"

The boys came to a halt and stared at me.

"A friend of mine just spent two weeks working side by side with Mother Teresa of Calcutta. Before my friend left to go to India she asked if there was anything for which I would like Mother to pray. Given she was going to be there on your birthday I asked if Mother could pray for you by name, Sean. The woman told me that she sat hand in hand with Mother Teresa and Mother Teresa said, 'Bless Sean Case on his birthday.'"

The boys were respectful, but they kept looking down the hall to their bedroom.

"Sean, did you hear me? Mother Teresa prayed for you by name."

To which Sean replied,

"Wow! That's great dad. Can we go play?"

I went stomping down the hall to my bedroom to stand before a four-foot icon of our Lord Jesus.

"Father, did you just see what happened with you son? I am not sure he was impressed that Mother Teresa prayed for him."

14

Quickly the Father spoke to my heart,

"So ... my son Jesus prays for him every day."

My babbling came to an immediate halt and I stood there dumb struck. I had never thought of this before. Romans 8:34 states: "Who is to condemn? It is Christ Jesus, who died, yes, who was raised, who is at the right hand of God, who indeed intercedes for us."

When this scripture is read in the original Greek, Jesus' intercession for us is in the present tense, meaning that RIGHT NOW he is interceding for you.

RIGHT NOW, before the Father's throne, the Lord Jesus stands as your High Priest with outstretched, pierced hands praying for you. RIGHT NOW, Jesus is praying for your relationships, your work, your finances, your struggles and concerns. RIGHT NOW, he is rejoicing over the grace which you have welcomed and adoring the Father for every blessing you have ever or will ever receive, blessings your mind does not have the space to perceive since they are so numerous. RIGHT NOW, Jesus is praying for you to have insight and revelation into the ways of the Kingdom. RIGHT NOW, he is praying that you will forgive those who have hurt you and be healed of that hurt. RIGHT NOW, he is praying for you to soak up all that you can from these 30 days to grow in the grace of prayer. Let your imagination wander – for what is Jesus praying for you, RIGHT NOW?

ACTION

- Become aware of Jesus standing before the Father on your behalf. Journal about any thoughts or feelings that come to your mind knowing that he is standing there for you.
- With whom and what will you share from today's lesson?

REFLECTION QUESTIONS

In the past, who was the most important person(s) you would want to have praying for you?

If there is anything for which you are glad to know that Jesus is interceding, what would it be?

15

What thoughts or feelings come to your mind when you think of Jesus standing before the Father on your behalf?

FURTHER READING

Hebrews 7:25

Hebrews 6:26

Hebrews 2:17

1 John 2:1

DAY
FOUR

Day 4: Talk to Your Dad

"Abba, Father," he said, "everything is possible for you. Take this cup from me. Yet not what I will, but what you will." Mark 14:36

MEDITATION

I was 18 years old and attending my first church conference. On the docket where famous, well-educated and degreed, inspirational speakers. With Bible, journal and pen in hand I was ready to soak up all that they had to give.

The day was structured with breakout sessions led by minor speakers and main assembly gatherings where the "big boy" keynote speakers would address the attendees.

The time came for the "Not to be Named" central keynote speaker. He was a Biblical Theologian whose books, thick, and one volume after another, I had been blessed to read. The title of his talk, *"Presenting God with Non-Offensive Titles"* or something like that. It was too many years ago for me to remember the exact title, but this title captures the essence of what he had to say. Fortunately, I was not aware of the title of his session before the speech began or else things could have been worse than what you are about to read.

The speaker started, *"In the name of the God who Created us, the One Who Redeemed us and the Spirit Who Sanctifies us"* and the great, enthusiastic crowd shouted, *"Amen,"* while I frowned, shock my head, and rolled my eyes.

The illustrious speaker went on to present how our titles for God need to transcend our culture and sexist constraints to be more inclusive given that many have been hurt by their fathers.

In what I am about to write I do not want to give the impression that I do not care about those who have been hurt by their dads. If you have been hurt by your dad, as a dad, I ask your forgiveness. I am so sorry that you do not have a positive, life-giving experience of your dad. I pray that you come to know the true Father of All who is loving and kind, gentle and caring and that your relationship with Him will heal your Father-Wound.

17

The one who is "Not to be Named" went on to speak of in great length of using titles for God that are non-offensive such as the above - the God who Created us, the One Who Redeemed us, and the Spirit Who Sanctifies us. After a good amount of time of the wheels in my head turning at a feverish rate, driven by an internal steam, I stood on my chair and yelled out,

"Father, repent! You have reduced God to a function. God is a person. He wants to be in a relationship with us. He is more than a function. Repent!"

At that point, rightfully so, I was assigned two personal body guards whom I did not need to pay. These men were so kind as to take my hand, help me off my chair, give me an escort to the doors of the conference center, leaving me with a firm request not to return. I do not want someone who is reading this to believe I handled this in the correct way. Jesus says that if you have a problem with your brother you are to go to him. I do not believe this means that you should include an auditorium full of people in your approach. Years later I meet "Not to be Named" and I asked his forgiveness. For some odd reason, he remembered me. May he rest in peace!

At that conference, I was standing for something that was foundational to the revelation of *Jesus' School of Prayer.* It is this - God is more than function and titles. God is a Father who will pay the greatest price, the death of His son, to be in relationship with us.

It is true that He is Lord. It is true that He is the Creator. It is true that He is Almighty. It is true that He is ... the list of truth goes on, but there is a superior truth which Jesus came and died to give us. It is the truth that He is our Father.

There is an old saying in the Church – *Lex orandi. Lex credendi*, which means *the rule of prayer is the rule of faith.* Let me clarify. How you pray tells us what you believe and what you believe determines how you pray. By listening to someone's prayer you find out what they really believe about God. *Lex orandi. Lex credendi.*

The setting for today's scripture, Mk 14:36, is Jesus is in the Garden of Gethsemane. The tortuous death that Jesus is about to face has just been made known to him. The forth coming events are so hideous that Jesus begins to sweat blood. In this moment of distress, his prayer will reveal to us what he believes, in the core of his being, as to whom it is that he is addressing his prayer.

"Abba, Father ..."

18

In this heartfelt address, we see deep into Jesus. What does he believe? He does not call on the All Powerful One who with no effort could come against those who are about to assail him. He does not call on the Just Judge whose sentence no one could deny. He calls on his *Abba*, his *Father*.

It should be noted that *Abba* is best transliterated as *Daddy* or *Papa*. Jesus does not reduce God to the function that he needs. He stands before *He Who Is, Yahweh*, as a son who pours out his heart to his *Daddy*, his *Papa*, his *Father*.

This is how we should address our prayer. In *Jesus' School of Prayer*, we do not begin our prayer with "Lord" though He is our Lord. *Jesus' School of Prayer* does not invite us to pray, "Dear God ..." *Jesus' School of Prayer* is to lead us into a relationship between *Abba* and His children.

How do you address your prayer? By listening to yourself you will find out what you truly believe about the God whom you are addressing.

Jesus taught in his *School of Prayer* that we are to address our prayer to the Father. The teaching of God's Fatherhood is so central to Jesus that it is something for which he was put to death.

In John 5:18 we read, "For this reason, they tried all the more to kill him; not only was he breaking the Sabbath, but he was even calling God his own Father, making himself equal with God."

In today's *Disciple's School of Prayer*, Jesus is inviting you to worship and call upon your *Abba*, your *Daddy*, your *Papa*, your *Father*.

PRAYER

Abba, my Father,
I am your child.
Papa, thank you for all you have done to reveal your love for me and to make it possible for me to be born again through the waters of baptism as your son, as your daughter.
Holy Spirit,
teach me to pray.
Change my heart so that I change my words of prayer so that they address my God as my *Abba*, my *Papa*, my *Father*.
Let me believe deep in my heart that Jesus has given me his *Abba* as my *Abba*, his *Daddy* as my *Daddy*.
In Jesus' name.

ACTION

- From your heart, simply talk to your Father about your life. Lay before your Father your joys and your sorrows, your hopes and your dreams, all the while saying, "*Abba, Daddy.*" You might find this uncomfortable, but push through to pray as Jesus. Write your prayer in your journal.
- With whom and what will you share from today's lesson?

REFLECTION QUESTIONS

To whom do you usually address your prayer and why?

What does it tell you about what you believe about God by the way you, personally, address God?

Before reading this mediation, did you know the centrality of the Fatherhood of God to in the teachings of the Lord Jesus?

How would you describe your relationship with God the Father?

What are the characteristic about Him, God, your *Abba*, that tell you that He is a good Father?

FURTHER READING

Romans 8:15-17

Galatians 4:6

John 14:6

Read Matthew 5,6, and 7 and circle all the times Jesus says, "your Father".

PRAYER HELP: Time & Environment

TIME

God, our Father, created us as both spirit and matter and these two must be kept in mind as one enters a time of encounter with the Trinity. We are not angels, pure spirit, and so we should not try to pray or act like them. We are sons and daughters of God with bodies and we will spend eternity in our resurrected bodies.

When it comes to the physical side of our person, two things should be considered when entering prayer: Time and Environment.

From the Genesis Days of Creation, we see that God marks out times and seasons. The seventh day *(literally to seven, meaning to cut off),* is the Sabbath, a day holy, cut off, unto the Lord. It is a day like no other day, a time like no other time. Later I will deal with the importance of keeping the Sabbath in our spiritual life. The Sabbath is a day for us to worship God and renew with Him our covenant. The Sabbath is a set time and teaches us how to live the other days of the week. The Sabbath teaches us the importance of set times of prayer, thus sanctifying time.

All of us have markers by which our day is structured. As a disciple of the Lord Jesus we should have marked out, cut out, times to be with him. In the early days of Christianity, we read from the Didache, written around 50 A.D., in section 8:2-3

Section 8:2. And do not pray as the hypocrites, but as the Lord commanded in his Gospel, pray thus: "Our Father, who art in Heaven, hallowed be thy Name, thy Kingdom come, thy will be done, as in Heaven so also upon earth; give us today our daily bread, and forgive us our debt as we forgive our debtors, and lead us not into trial, but deliver us from the Evil One. For thine is the power and the glory forever."

Section 8:3. Pray thus three times a day. Traditionally, those times are morning, evening and night prayer. Psalm 55:17 reads, *"Evening, morning and noon I cry out in distress, and he hears my voice."* With these admonitions in mind we should set and commit to three times a day for us to pray – morning, evening and night. You might start with 15 minutes for morning and evening prayer. I would recommend no less than 15 minutes as you will never grow in a life of prayer if you pray less than 15 minutes. As time progresses and you mature in the life of the Holy Spirit, do not be surprised if one of your 15-minute prayer times turns into half an hour and a half an hour turns into an hour. The time that will usually expand is the time that works best with your inner clock, your circadian rhythm. For some people, morning prayer is when their mind is the most clear and available to the Lord (this is me) and it is the best time for extended prayer.

For others, their brain is still waking and it is hard for them to pray in the morning. If you have a hard time with your brain waking in the morning then I suggest that you use rote prayers that honor God and establish Him as Lord as you go into your day *(Morning Offering and a simple reading of a devotional)*. Though your mind might not feel that it is absorbing the reading, your spirit is drinking from God's Word. A mistake that people make is thinking that they are just a mind and forgetting that they are also a spirit. The spirit can absorb when the mind cannot. It is this simple – if you want a tan, get in the sun. You don't need to analyze the sun to get a tan. You just need to expose yourself to its rays. It is the same with the Word of God. You will be surprised when the Word you have read comes to your mind when you need it. I tell people this, "If the seed is never planted you will never see a tree." Plant the seed of the Word, reading it, and trust that it will grow in your heart.

For your morning prayer time, you might need to set the alarm and wake before your usual waking time. This is a worthy sacrifice which will hold out rewards in this life and the next.

Your evening prayer time might be right after the dishes are done and the house is settling in for the night.

Night prayer should be a conscious decision to be done, not in bed, but right before one goes under the covers. It need not be as long as the other times.

All these times, of course, include the *Our Father*.

If you are a parent, what a great witness it will be to your children to see you committed to prayer at different times throughout the day.

ENVIRONMENT

I love it when a restaurant not only has tasty food, but the right ambiance. The music, the lighting, the decorations, and the food add to the experience. We are sensory beings and our senses help us to pray. This is why Catholic churches are filled with icons and statues and the smells of beeswax candles and incense. It is the ambiance of the heavenly in the earth. We need the same in our personal prayer time. We need a quiet place that will not pull us away from the One Who Longs to Be with Us. We need a comfortable chair so we are not distracted by being uncomfortable, or maybe kneeling helps you to stay focused so you can

23

encounter the Lord of the Encounter. Certain types of music help me to pray and maybe music will help you. Some people pray best when they walk. The pace of their walk and the beauty of the earth pulls them into the Presence. Light a candle and sit before an icon of our Lord or our Lady and this helps their heart come into the presence of the Lord.

Be aware of your environment and purposely choose a place which helps you to be with your *Father*, your *Abba,* your *Daddy.*

Day 5: In Jesus' Name

"Whatever you ask in my name, this I will do, that the Father may be glorified in the Son. If you ask me anything in my name, I will do it."
John 14:13-14

MEDITATION

My children were playing in the front yard and I was sitting on the porch. I could hear barking from down the street. I turned to see five huge Rottweilers running in their direction. There was not enough time for my kid's little legs to get to safety, so I did what a dad should do. I ran into the yard and placed myself between my children and the now crouched down dogs who were angrily barking at me. My arms were spread out and I was ushering my kids to the porch were my wife was waiting to snatch them up. As I moved, the dogs moved closer. My heart was racing. The dogs started lunging at me and then retreating. I am not going tell you how I wrestled each to the ground and left all five whimpering as they ran away. That would be a lie. I used the only weapon I had.

I stepped forward, straightened my spine, and with a pointed finger, I jutted it at the dogs and yelled,

"In the name of Jesus, I commend you to be at peace!"

My finger must have been loaded with Kingdom Power. Immediately, the dogs quieted and stood still, looking at me. I am not lying!

I then commanded,

"In the name of Jesus, GO!" forcefully pointing in the direction I wanted them to leave.

The crazy dogs obeyed and went running off with not one bark.

Everything we need is in the name of Jesus, everything. Do you know this? Do you believe this? His name is the name to which everything must bend. Do you believe that everything must bend to the name of Jesus, who is Lord? There is power in the name of Jesus. Disciple of the Lord Jesus, we need to recover a great love for and new faith in his name. His name, Jesus, is than name above all names. We have no idea of the power of the tongue that wields this name. His name is so fierce that every demon

25

and even Satan himself is subject to the mouth that speaks this name, the name of Jesus.

The utterance of the name, accompanied with faith, causes heaven to open and pour forth. Nothing is impossible to the one who uses the name of Jesus. Were you looking for the key to all of heaven's treasures? It is the name of Jesus.

I have studied many of the major religions of the world. Their gods demand this and that and then they will turn to the petitioner. It amazes me that the True and Living God of Israel, *Yahweh*, our *Father*, our Abba, our *Daddy*, our *Papa*, has made it so simple that all one needs to do is whisper the name, *"Jesus,"* and all heaven turns to the one who has spoken, with faith, the name. Your *Abba* so loves you and knows that you are so small that He has made it so a child can marshal heaven to its aid by the proclamation of one word – JESUS!

Throughout the years as I have traveled the U.S. preaching the Gospel of the Kingdom, I ask people how we end prayer. I invite the assembly to yell it out. The response is always the same. It is a loud, "AMEN!" I then go on to instruct the Church from *Jesus' School of Prayer*. Jesus clearly taught that whatever we ask in his name he would do and that we were to ask in his name. The ending of prayer is, *"in Jesus' name."* Notice when you go to Mass how the priest will always pray in the name of Jesus. "Amen" means we agree with the person leading the prayer and we make their prayer our prayer.

Our prayer is to the Father, in Jesus' name.

I really want to emphasize this. If we are disciples of Jesus then we need to pray as he taught which might not be the way we are used to praying. He is the Master and we are the disciples. His way is this:

Our prayer is to the Father, in Jesus' name.

Now, why would this be so important to pray to the Father in Jesus' name? There are many gods to whom your prayer could be addressed, but no other God is Father. By praying to the Father all other gods must step aside for the true God.

Why must we pray in the name of Jesus? In the ancient world to do something in someone's name implied the person whose name you were using was there, present, doing whatever you were doing in their name. To pray in the name of Jesus brings Jesus into your prayer and makes that prayer acceptable to the Father.

What I am about to write might be an offense to your ego, your fallen, carnal man that wants things in the way it wants them and it wants them in that way right now.

Jesus taught in John 14:6, "I am the way, the truth, and the life. No one comes to the Father but through me."

Without Jesus, you cannot come into the presence of the Father. It is because of Jesus that you have access to the throne of grace. You, in and of yourself, cannot approach God the Father. Many of us think that anyone can just mosey into the presence of God and God has to hear them. Yikes! These people are in for a surprise. In the Old Testament, a truth was enacted for us. In the tabernacle of Moses, the Father dwelt in the Holy of Holies over the Ark of the Covenant. There was a veil that separated the presence of God from all that happened on the other side of the veil. Once a year, the High Priest, and only the High Priest, on the Day of Yom Kippur, was able to pierce the veil and come before the glory of God. If anyone else entered, they would be struck dead. Jesus, by his death and for those who have faith in him, rent in two the veil to heaven and made it so that we may approach, in his name, in his person, before the Father. His name is the door opener to heaven. His name, alone gives us access to the Father and without his name we have no access. It is his name that gives you the right to come before the Father. No one can approach the Father in their name alone. His name is necessary for access.

In the ancient world to use someone's name also meant you had their authority and power. Hear this clearly – when you pray in the name of Jesus you have his authority and you have his power.

Let's review: the name of Jesus brings his presence, his authority and his power.

O, disciple, why would you not pray in his name? Enter *Jesus' School of Prayer*. From now on let there never be a prayer you pray that is not to the Father, in the name of Jesus.

I have to add one more thing about the story of me facing off the dogs and the power of the name of Jesus. I told that story to my daughter Rebekah when she was about seven years old. One day she was in her bed room and a pesky fly would not leave her alone. She swatted and moved and it moved with her. Finally, she pulled out her finger, directed it toward the fly and sternly proclaimed, "In Jesus name!" and the fly went zooming out of her room. You might call it coincidence, but I call it child-like faith.

PRAYER

Abba, Father,
thank you for the powerful name of Jesus.
Thank you that all that you are and all that you have is available to me because of that name.
Holy Spirit,
teach me to pray to the Father, in Jesus name.
Lord Jesus,
increase my faith in the power of your name that I might walk in your presence, authority, and power.
Abba, my Father,
I ask this in Jesus' name.
Amen

ACTION

- Set a goal for today to pray at least seven times to the Father in the name of Jesus. Get used to the Jesus Pattern for Prayer.
- With whom and what will you share from today's lesson?

REFLECTION QUESTIONS

What did you learn from today's lesson?

Why do we need to pray "in the name of Jesus?"

What does praying in the name of Jesus imply?

FURTHER READING

John 16:24

John 15:16

John 16:23-24

Colossians 3:17

Acts 4:12

Philippians 2:6-11

Day 6: The Greatest Gift

If you then, though you are evil, know how to give good gifts to your children, how much more will your Father in heaven give the Holy Spirit to those who ask him! Luke 11:13

MEDIATION

I admit that of all that I will write in the *Disciple's School of Prayer,* this will be the most fun, for it will be about the person with whom I have been on an adventure since I was 16 years old, my constant, abiding companion and friend, the Holy Spirit. I pray that you will come to know my friend and you will invite and integrate him into every aspect of your life. I pray the *Disciple's School of Prayer* will introduce you to him or you will come to know him, somehow, someway in some other way. A *Life in the Spirit Seminar* is a great way to get to know my friend, the Holy Spirit, but they are a rare these days. Another great tool is www.thewildgooseisloose.com. It is a 14 week course by Franciscan friar, Father Dave Pivonka, which will introduce you to the Holy Spirit, his gifts and his way of life.

You can also go to www.BrendanCase.com, hover over "Tools for Growth", and go through my *School of the Holy Spirit.* Lastly, I would welcome the opportunity to pray with you for the Baptism of the Holy Spirit – 480.313.3990.

Before we go any further, right now, just pray, "Come, Holy Spirit!" Let your heart say this prayer for a while.

In *Jesus' School of Prayer,* he instructs his disciples that they need to worship in the Spirit, that we need to pray in the Spirit. I want to tell you about how I came to meet my friend and came to pray in the Spirit. You can read a more in-depth account in my book, **Relentless Pursuit**.

I was 16 years old and on my way home from the Friday night football game. A year before, I had given my life to the Lord Jesus and started going to Mass on a weekly basis. As I was driving I took out my rosary and began the Glorious Mysteries. I came to the third mystery, the Descent of the Holy Spirit on Pentecost. I really didn't know anything about Pentecost, but as I prayed, *"Hail Mary, full of ..."* words came out of my mouth that were not English. *"Hail Mary ..."* my words became less and less as this other language took over. I did not know what was happening. I pulled to the side of the road, ran out of my truck, and the words continued to pour out. In fear, I fell on my knees, threw up my hands and said the only thing I could say in English, *"Jesus, save me!"* and he did. That night my life changed. It was if I was a new person, as they say, born again.

After that night, the hunger for God grew and grew. I would find myself, alone, out in the desert, spending the whole weekend in prayer. Sister Gerard had given me a Bible. Now, when I read, it was if it was written right to me and I understood things that I had never been taught, which, when I read before, I did not understand. I longed to go to Mass and receive Jesus' body and blood, the Eucharist. I was alive!

Years later I attended a charismatic prayer meeting and discovered there were other Catholics who had a similar encounter with God. They explained to me that I had received the grace of the Baptism of the Holy Spirit. I had received the sacrament of Baptism when I was a few days old. That is when the Holy Spirit came to live in me. Now, I had come to live in him. I came to see that I had experienced Pentecost as if I was one of the disciples in the upper room on that 50th day after the resurrection of the Lord Jesus when the Holy Spirit formed the Church. I, like them, now knew him. I, like them, met him and he was as real, if not more real, than anyone I had ever known. I, like them, could sense his presence with me. I found a people who were filled with the Holy Spirit. Their worship was amazing. They would sing and praise God freely from their hearts. Many would dance and others would clap. For hours, we would be lost in His presence, praying the tongues which was my own personal language that I received from the Father that night in the desert. As we worshipped, we would raise our hands in praise and fall on our faces in adoration. We were worshipping, like Jesus said, in Spirit and in truth. We were the people of whom Jesus spoke who had rivers of living water flowing from our bellies, from the center of our being; the Spirit of God was pouring forth.

The disciple who has been formed in *Jesus' School of Prayer* knows from Jesus that the spiritual life is not a matter of trying hard. The disciples of Jesus know that the spiritual life is about surrender -- allowing the Holy Spirit to live through them, to pray through them, to serve through them. O, what a glorious freedom to live in and by the Holy Spirit instead of one's own will power!

In Day Three of *Disciple's School of Prayer* we learned that Jesus is praying for us. Let me show you for what he is asking of your *Abba* for you. He is asking, he is praying for you to receive more of the Holy Spirit. Above all, your *Father,* your *Papa* wants you to have more of the Holy Spirit. Jesus is praying we might have the greatest gift of all, God's life living in us, the Holy Spirit. For us to have this gift is the reason he died and rose.

Yes, he died and rose that our sins might be washed away. But let us not forget that they are washed away so the Spirit can dwell in us. Hear me, you have received a gift from your *Father, Abba*, by the death and resurrection of Jesus that is greater than the gift of heaven. You have, by Jesus death and resurrection, a Person who lives in you always, even the Spirit of truth.

This Holy Spirit, the gift of your *Father*, wants you to join him in bringing forth the Kingdom of God in the earth. He has come to you to be the power of your proclamation that the Kingdom of God is at hand and the power that allows you to demonstrate the presence of this Kingdom through signs and wonders. Read the Acts of the Apostles and the lives of the Saints and know that the Spirit of God wants to do in you and through you what he did to them and through them -- no less. Do not discount what I have just written, for it is true about you. In these days, the Lord Jesus is looking for a people who will surrender to the movement of the Holy Spirit to bring forth the Kingdom, on earth as it is in heaven. He is ready to use you to heal the sick, to cleanse the leper, to raise the dead, and to cast out demons. Yes, it is you. He is ready to use you! Believe that the Spirit is going to use you and do not continue in your unbelief that it must be someone else.

What adventures must he have in store for you if you just surrender and learn of his ways? Most of us have never been instructed in the ways of the Spirit so we do not know how to move in the Spirit. I recommend to you a free book on my website that will help you to discover the manifestations of the Spirit, the charismatic gifts, and how they work. Go to my website, now, and download this book that will open your eyes. www.BrendanCase.com. Click on "Tools for Growth". Download **The Key to the Charismatic Renewal in the Catholic Church** by Monsignor Vincent Walsh. Get ready for an amazing read.

O, disciple of Jesus, why would you wait one more moment? My friend wants to be your friend, your Constant, Abiding Companion. Cry out with a longing beyond what you have ever longed –

COME, HOLY SPIRIT! MORE OF YOU, HOLY SPIRIT, MORE!

PRAYER

Abba, Father,
thank you for all you have done for me in giving all that Jesus gave that I might receive your greatest gift, the Holy Spirit.
Holy Spirit,
I welcome you.

You are my Constant, Abiding Companion and now I want to live my life with you.
I want you, Holy Spirit, to be my friend.
Teach me to pray.
Jesus,
You said you would baptize us in the Holy Spirit.
Jesus,
baptize me in the Holy Spirit like the Apostles on the day of Pentecost and send me forth as a witness to your resurrection, proclaiming and demonstrating the Kingdom of God.
I am ready, Holy Spirit, I am ready.
Come, Holy Spirit, come!
In Jesus' name.
Amen

ACTION

- Read the Acts of the Apostles and as you read, pray, "Lord Jesus, do that in my life."
- With whom and what will you share from today's lesson?

REFLECTION QUESTIONS

How would you describe to someone who the Holy Spirit is?

How would you describe your relationship with the Holy Spirit?

What do you know about the Baptism of the Holy Spirit?

What do you think or how do you feel about the gift of tongues?

FURTHER READING

John 14:16

Luke 11:9-13

John 7:37-39

Acts of the Apostles 1:5; 8

Day 7: Hearing the Voice

At that time Jesus came from Nazareth in Galilee and was baptized by John in the Jordan. Just as Jesus was coming up out of the water, he saw heaven being torn open and the Spirit descending on him like a dove. And a voice came from heaven: "You are my Son, whom I love; with you I am well pleased." Mark 1:9-11

MEDITATION

It was a Saturday night and I was 15 years old. That night we watched a movie that changed my life. The movie was *The Miracle of Our Lady of Fatima*. That night I came to believe that God was personal and available. Fatima is the story of three Portuguese peasant children who on May 13, 1917, started receiving visitations from Mary, the Mother of Jesus. From that night on, every night I would kneel in my room, saying the rosary as our Lady requested. As I prayed, I would open my eyes, every now and then, to see if she, Our Lady, was there, appearing to me. My child-like faith believed that if it could happen to those children it could happen to me and that same faith resides in me to this day. I expect and am open to encounters with God and I expect to hear His voice.

At that same time of seeing the movie, I had come upon a cave in the desert mountains not far from my house. I would go to that cave to spend weekends, reading the Word, with journal in hand, listening for my Father, my *AhDah*, to speak to me. By myself, in that desert cave, I did learn to tune my heart to hear His still, small, familiar voice.

There are three principles in the *School of Prayer* regarding hearing the voice of the Father:

- God is our Father and as our Father, he wishes to speak to us.
- What is true for Jesus is also true for us because we are in Jesus. Since Jesus heard from his Father, we, by the gift of the Holy Spirit, can also hear from him.
- Prayer is a dialogue between and soul and God. It is not meant to be a monologue.

For most believers, prayer is a monologue, rather than a dialogue. How it must disappoint the Father that when we come to pray we do not leave time for Him to speak. Hear this, Beloved of the Son, your Father is waiting for the next time you are to spend with him and he has much he wants to press upon your soul in so many ways.

With these three principles in mind, how then can our prayer become a dialogue?

First, allow faith to rise in your heart that God is your Father and as your Father, your *Abba,* your *Daddy,* your *Papa,* he wants to speak to you, his child. One of the traps in the spiritual life is to believe that certain things are reserved for the few, mainly, the Saints. Most of us would say, *"I am not a Saint, so why would God speak to me?"* This statement brings unbelief into our hearts. Banish this unbelief with this truth: you might not be a Saint, but because of baptism, you are a son or daughter of God and he is your Father. Being his is enough to hear from him.

Second, you probably just need to learn some listening skills that apply to the life of your spirit. Let me share a few helpful tools.

Let me recommend my 30-day series, *Hearing the Voice of God.* Every day you will listen to a 20-minute teaching and receive a worksheet with notes and spiritual exercises to enable you to hear your Father's voice. Go to www.BrendanCase.com. Hover your cursor over "Tools for Growth."

Here are the **H.O.W.S.** of how the Father speaks to His children:

Heart – your Father will speak in a still, small, familiar voice in your heart.
Others – He will speak His word to you through others.
World Circumstances – He will use the events of your life to speak to you.
Sacred Revelation – He will speak through the Word of God and through the Tradition and Magisterium of the Church.

I would also recommend that you journal your prayer time. For me, journaling is praying at the point of a pen. When I journal, I literally write out my conversation with God. I write what he says and my response, or vice versa. I read his Word and allow thoughts to flow from my pen, trusting that he is speaking to me. I have found that many times God speaks in puzzle pieces, meaning that he will only give me a little at a time. When I put these pieces together, then I can see a bigger picture. Many times, these pieces are revealed over a period of days or months.

In the front of your journal establish an index. Do not write in the first six pages. Begin numbering your journal for page 1 on page 7. After your prayer time, ask the Holy Spirit to summarize your encounter in a few words. Every Sunday review your index and see if there are any pieces that might fit together. On the first Friday of the month, review a month's worth of your index, looking for the pieces that might fit together.

In all this, hear, O disciple of Jesus, your *Abba* wants to speak to you and your prayer time needs to include moments when his word can break into your spirit.

PRAYER

Father,
whose presence is ever near,
here I am, ready to hear your voice.
Speak, Father, my *Abba,*
I am listening.
Lord Jesus,
Thank you for bringing me into the same relationship which you have with the Father.
Holy Spirit,
teach me to pray. Increase my faith that my Father wants to speak to me and teach me how to hear His voice.
In Jesus' name.
Amen

ACTION

- Go to www.BrendanCase.com and find the *Hearing the Voice of God Series* and mark it as a favorite so you can go through it after you complete *Disciple's School of Prayer*.
- With whom and what will you share from today's lesson?

REFLECTION QUESTIONS

What do you think or feel about the idea that the Father wants to speak to you?

Do you think that your Father would speak to you? If you doubt that he would speak to you, what are your doubts?

Have you ever heard the voice of God?

How could you make room to hear the voice of God in your daily prayer time?

FURTHER READING

1 Kings 19:11-13

1 Samuel 3:7-11

Psalm 85:8

John 10:27

Day 8: Entering with Thanksgiving

Taking the five loaves and the two fish and looking up to heaven, he gave thanks and broke them. Then he gave them to the disciples to distribute to the people. Lk 9:16

MEDITATION

It was after the 5pm, Saturday Mass and I was preaching in a small town. Father invited me to the hall for a Tamale Dinner to raise funds for the teens. I made my way around the room meeting different members of the parish, inviting them to come to the Parish Mission I was preaching which would follow that week.

"Do you believe in the Baptism of the Holy Spirit," asked a man about my age.

I quickly responded with great glee, "You better believe in it! That is why I am here this week."

"Do you believe in speaking in tongues?" was his next inquiry.

With the same excitement I replied, "That is why I am here this week. Are you coming to the Mission this coming week?"

"I am not from this church. I am a Pentecostal Minister and so is my dad," to whom he pointed.

Gary, my new Pentecostal friend, and his parents came to every night of the Parish Mission. At the end of the Mission they shared they had never seen such a movement of God with such ease. This has been one of the greatest compliments I have ever received when it comes to my ministry.

That mission week, I spent all my "off time" with Gary and we grew in our brotherhood and friendship. During that week, I also saw Gary interact with his dad and heard Gary speak of his dad with amazing respect and fondness. Towards the end of the week I asked Gary what he admired about his dad. There were many things he shared, but one thing he said will never leave me. This one thing he said about his dad was the one thing I wanted to be for my children.

Gary shared that from his childhood until that present day, every morning he awoke to the sound of his father praising God and praying in tongues. When I heard this description of Gary's dad I wanted to live in that way for my children. I wanted them to awake to the sound of their dad praising and thanking God.

If there is anything that is markedly different about the Charismatic Renewal (called the Renewal of the Spirit in some parts of the world) as compared to other spiritualities, it is that of verbally praising God. When one goes to a charismatic prayer meeting, he will hear a cacophony of believers raising up their voices, speaking out the praises of God:

"Praise you, Jesus!"
Thank you, Lord!
I love you, Father!
Glory to you, O Lord!
I bless you! I praise you! I adore you!
You are my God!
Glory to you, O Lord!
Alleluia!

Praising, thanking, and blessing God is at the center of a life in the Holy Spirit. For some people, this is overwhelming and uncomfortable. I have a question: who would make it uncomfortable for us when we are in the midst of disciples who are praising God? Would it be the Holy Spirit or the evil spirit?

When you stop and think about it, what is the reason your Father, your Daddy, gave you a tongue and gave you a voice? Is it not to be used, first, to speak forth His praise? Is it not for you to say out loud, "Thank you, my Abba, for all you are and do for me?" Were we not given a voice so that we could, first, like Jesus, look up to heaven, and give thanks? You have been created to give praise and worship to your Father. This is the first and primary reason for your existence. Our culture's instruction is that your life's purpose is self-fulfillment. No, disciple, do not fall for this lie. Your purpose is to praise God, not to be self-fulfilled, but to be self-emptied in the pouring out of self in worship of Him. The challenge is to enact your purpose, praising and thanking God, in your times of prayer and throughout the day. Let us, O disciple of Jesus, become ones from whose lips these words easily flow forth,

"Thank you, Father!"
"I am blessed and I know Who is it that has blessed me. It is not the universe. It is my Father."
"Praise God!"

Will there be people who give you strange looks? Of course, there will be eyes that roll when you speak forth His praise. Let this not be your concern. The fear of man has held back so many souls from being who they are and doing what they are called to do in the Kingdom. Let this not be you. Stand tall and proud that you are a son or daughter of your Abba and you are grateful to make His praise known. In doing this you are also calling forth in the souls that hear their purpose.

What would your life be like if you started your day giving thanks to the Father? I have applied the way of Gary's dad to my life. I bought myself a Buddhist bracelet, they are called Mala Beads, and consecrated them to Jesus. I call them Gratitude Beads. My bracelet has 33 beads. The 33 beads stand for that for which I am most grateful, the earthly life of Jesus, which was 33 years. Every morning I start my day by speaking, out loud, in the presence of my family, things like this,

"Father, thank you for your love.
Jesus, thank you for your love.
Holy Spirit, thank you for your love.
Father, thank you for the soft chair on which I am sitting.
Thank you for running water.
Thank you, Father, that I am baptized, that I am your son.
Thank you for gasoline.
Thank you, Father, for all the blessings you constantly pour into my life. There are more blessing that I receive that I will never know of than the ones which I do know."
Thank you, Father.
Praise you, Father.
You are so good to me.
I love you, Father."

Disciple, let your morning prayer and other times of prayer begin with praise. In the Old Testament, God the Father came to meet with the people at the Tent of Meeting. This Tent was enclosed by a linen wall which only had one opening through which to pass into the enclosure to enter the actual Tent of Meeting. The twelve tribes of Israel were encamped around the House of God and were assigned their places. The tribe which was commanded to pitch their tents before the linen gate, opening to the enclosure, was the tribe of Judah. Judah, in Hebrew, means praise. Hear this, Follower of the Messiah. It is through praise that you must pass to enter the presence of God. This is why we begin the Mass with the Gloria. We start with praise. In this ancient prayer which begins, "Glory to God in the highest," do we not sing out, "We praise you, we bless you, we adore you, we glorify you." This ancient hymn is filled with one praise after another. Next time, be aware of what you are proclaiming as the words slip forth from your lips.

41

To help you to grow in your vocabulary of praise, I have written a book which I recommend to you.

Go to Amazon.com and search for Manual of Praise.

I wrote this book for me so that I could enter more fully into the praise of God. The book includes:

Praise Phrases
The Scriptural Names of God and where they are found
The Scriptural Names of the Father and where they are found
The Scriptural Names of Jesus and where they are found
The Scriptural Names of the Spirit and where they are found
The Hebrew Names of God and where they are found
Adjectives for Praising God
Litanies and Akathist of Praise
Psalms of Praise

O Disciple, today, use your voice for that which it was created. Use your voice to worship your Papa, out loud, in the presence of His people.

PRAYER

Father, my Abba,
how glorious, how wonderful, how amazing you are.
I love you. I adore you. I glorify your name.
Thank you for all you have done for me and all you will do for me.
I stand amazed at how blessed I am.
I have received so many blessings that I will never be able to thank you for all of them.
Thank you!
Holy Spirit,
teach me how to pray.
Help me to enter more deeply into a life of praising and thanking my *Daddy* for His generosity and mercy toward me. I want to become a person who is known for gratitude, especially by the Host of Heaven.
In Jesus' name.

ACTION

- In your journal, write on one page "Praise" and on another page "Thanksgiving." Praise is for who God is. Thanksgiving is for what God has done. Now, make a list under each. This will become your cheat sheet for when you begin your prayer time with praise and thanksgiving. Also, please order my book from Amazon, *Manual of Praise*. I just flip back and forth through it and read off the names of God, praise phrases, and adjectives for God.

- With whom and what will you share from today's lesson?

REFLECTION QUESTIONS

What are some things for which you are grateful to the Father?

How is praising and thanking God a part of your daily prayer?

How do feel about thanking God out loud?

What would be added to your life if you started your day giving thanks to the Father for all He is and all He does?

FURTHER READING

Psalm 100

Hebrews 13:15

Psalm 34:1-2

1 Thessalonians 5:16-18

Luke 1:46-55

Philippians 4:6-7

Day 9: Confidence in a Loving, Hearing Father

They took away the stone. Then Jesus looked up and said, "Father, I thank you that you have heard me. I knew that you always hear me, but I said this for the benefit of the people standing here, that they may believe that you sent me."
John 11:41-42

MEDITATION

In 1996 the clear voice of the Father spoke to my heart. I was a Life TEEN youth minister. The youth group had grown immensely and we had a solid core team of leaders in a variety of components for the youth ministry program. I loved doing what I was doing, but the Spirit was tugging at my heart to do something beyond the local Church. I was also being called by Church leadership, as they said, "to go preach." This meant that I would no longer have a parish supporting me financially. As a believer in Jesus, who surrendered his life to his Lordship, I knew that I had to seek the Father's will. This is what the Father spoke to my heart in that still, small voice.

"If you take care of my house, I will take care of you."

His house is the Church. He promised that if I would take care of his Church that he would take care of my family (my two sons and me). I knew that I was called to a life trusting in him for everything, meaning, everything. Did I have permission, then, to just sit around and watch TV? NO! I needed to be about caring for his house, his people, the Church.

There were two questions to be asked, though:

1) Was it really the Father's will and therefore a promise from him?
2) Who did I really believe this Father to be?

As to the first question. I went to my prayer community and asked for their discernment. These were strong, committed, mature believers to whom I had given my life and they had given me their lives. We had become, because of Jesus, family. I trusted these brothers and sisters. They knew my call and gifting and they would seek God's will above my comfort. I also went to my Spiritual Director for the same. At the time, I was not married, else I would have first gone to my wife. Both my community and my spiritual director believed that this was indeed a word from the Father to my heart. I now knew that it was my Father's will for me to trust him to take care of my house as I took care of his.

45

Now, for the second question which, I believe, is really the most important question. In whom was I putting my trust to provide and care for my sons and me? Here is a *Brendan Dictum:*

What you believe about the Fatherhood of God will determine how much you can trust Him.

For a moment, I invite you to stop and think about what Jesus believed about God being his Father. I mean what I said.

STOP AND DO NOT READ ANY MORE.

What confidence must have filled his heart in everything which he did in his life because Jesus knew that his Father loved him and was with him. When he stood before Satan in the desert, hungry and weak after 40 days of fasting, tempted, but needing to battle, he stood there confident that he was the Father's son. When his mother told him that the newly married couple was out of wine, she, knowing that he could do something, approached with a request. He looked at the huge jugs filled with water and with confidence, knew that all he had to do is say *"Father!"* and the water would become wine. Why would water obey? Because he was the son and God was his father. The disciples headed across the lake to the other shore and Jesus, in the dark of the night, stepped onto the water, walking on its surface, completely confident that he would not sink as he strode above the deepest depth because he is the Father's son. When Jesus faced an angry crowd, he faced it as a son who was confident that his father loved him. When beaten, spit upon, and punched, he did so with an unwavering surety of who he was, his father's son. Through eyes clouded by blood, gazing out as he hung, suspended between heaven and earth, on the Cross, he could see a clear vision from his heart — I am confident of this — "I am His son and he loves me and always hears my prayer." When his eyes opened in the dark hole of the tomb and he came forth risen from the dead, he came forth and stood before creation with the same confidence which rose in his heart at every other moment of his life. "I am His son whom he loves and hears."

Now, let us consider ourselves. As disciples, we believe that He, God our Father, is All-powerful and All-knowing. We believe that He is good and that He only wills and does good. Here comes the hard part. The afore-mentioned attributes of God are easy to believe. But what about the attributes that apply to me?

The next things about God are things which relate to you, and you must muster up trust to say, *"Yes, this is what I believe about my Father!"*

46

I believe He is an amazingly good, kind, and generous *AhDah.*

(AhDah - This is what I call God, my Father. It is the heartfelt way I address Him which is beyond a title. It comes from my daughter, Rebekah. When Rebekah was a wee little girl she would call me, AhDah. My heart broke the day she called me dad. It is from her tender heart toward me that I was given my name by which to speak to the Father from my heart.)

I believe that I live under the blessing of His hand and it pleases Him to give me His Kingdom. I believe that my *Father,* my *Abba,* my *Papa,* my *AhDah* longs to bless me and with this I can be confident that He hears my prayer. My *AhDah* hears me every time I pray. He never turns a deaf ear. He is never too busy or finds something more important. My *AhDah* does not think that there are prayers that I pray that are important and prayers that I pray that are trivial. My *AhDah* cares just as much about my need to have money for gas as He cares about my need to walk in holiness. Every hair on my head is just as precious to my *AhDah* as my soul. I am precious to Him, all of me and all of my life. This might sound like I have gone too far, but which part of your children's lives do you love the most and care about the most? Do you not care about every aspect of their lives? I want their souls to be saved and for them to have something to eat.

There is an unfortunate truth for many a believer that holds them back from being a disciple. It is the wounds which came from their parents, whether it was purposeful on their parents' part or not. These wounds weaken confidence in God because our parents, if you will, are our first gods to us. We learn from these hurts a lie that those in power over us cannot be trusted. We then project this on to God, our Father. The second unfortunate truth is our lack of maturity in the spiritual life. We pray and we pray for something we intensely desire, and our prayer is not answered in the way that we want it to be answered. After this, our confidence that God is a good Father greatly wanes and our heart is wounded. For both wounds, we need healing. For the first wound we are to practice forgiveness of our parents; for the second wound, we need to repent of judging God because we found ourselves to be wiser than him.

O Disciple, is it not time at this very moment to see all the grandeur of who your *Abba* is and what he has made you to be as his son or daughter? Is it not time, then, to stand in confidence when you pray, knowing that you are always heard?

PRAYER

Father,
I do thank you that you always hear my prayer.
Never once has one of my prayers not been heard by you because you are a good Father.
Whenever I say *Father* you direct all of heaven to my aid.
I have your heart for your heart is consumed in love for me.
Holy Spirit,
teach me how to pray.
When I stand before the Father give me the grace to stand in confidence before him as a son or daughter.
Expand my heart to see He who is my *Papa*, my *Father.*
In Jesus' name.
Amen

ACTION

- In your journal, make a list of all the times in your life or in your family that God has taken care of you.
- With whom and what will you share from today's lesson?

REFLECTION QUESTIONS

When you believe the things which I just wrote about my relationship with God, are they true about your relationship with God?

Do you have confidence that the Father hears you whenever you pray about whatever you are praying?

What do you think causes any weakness in your heart in believing that God is a good Father and that He longs to bless you?

FURTHER READING

Isaiah 30:18

Psalm 34:8

Jeremiah 17:7-8

Numbers 6:24-26

Philippians 4:19

PRAYER HELP: Prayer is a Dialogue

It is important to remember that prayer is not a task to be accomplished, but a time when a relationship is built and deepened between us and God. Handling prayer as a task is a common trap into which many a soul falls and therefore those souls never mature or enter into the blessings their Father has for them.

Another trap is to believe that prayer is the time I do all the talking and God does all the listening. This is the way of prayer for most believers : we talk, God listens. I think it is probably a universal truth that we naturally avoid relationships where the other does all the talking and we cannot get a word in edgewise. Why do we avoid such encounters? Because this is not a relationship. A relationship is reciprocal and mutual. Prayer is relationship and, therefore, it must be a dialogue, involving two who are reciprocal and mutual. When we do all the talking and God does all the listening then our prayer is a monologue, with us in control.

True prayer is a dialogue as it allows for God to speak and us to hear. As with any relationship, one of the persons involved must initiate the conversation. For the Christian, it is permissible to speak to God about that which is on one's heart, but there also needs be, if the relationship is mutual, time for God to converse with our spirit. For most, the thought of God speaking to them is remote for they believe that this is something that would only happen for the few, the Saints. Since God is our Father, he wishes to speak to all his children, not just some chosen few. It is this simple. Is it a good dad or bad dad that does not speak to his children? A bad dad does not talk to his kids. Since God is a good Father, the Father of all fathers, it stands to truth that He wants to communicate with us regarding His will and His love.

In our time of prayer, we should allow for God to speak. For me, I say from my heart, "Speak, Lord, your servant is listening."

With pen in hand, I then write down what comes to my spirit, trusting that the Father is speaking to me. Mostly, He speaks to me of His love. He also gives me direction as to His will. There are two things which seem to be usual about His voice:

1) It is a still, small voice. It is soft and interior; therefore, one must make space for quiet in his life to be able to hear. (1 Kings 19:11-13)
2) It is a familiar voice. God's voice will probably sound like your voice in your head. Why? Because God is using you, your thoughts, to speak to you, which means it will sound like you. (1 Samuel 3:7-11)

We should also allow for times when we allow Him to initiate the conversation. How, then, does God direct a conversation with a soul? The most common way is through the use of the Word in the disciple's prayer time. This method is called *Lectio Divina*. *Lectio* is a flow of conversation

Lectio - To Read. God speaks as we take up a passage and read it slowly three or four times noticing what concepts or words are ministering to our heart.

Meditatio – To Meditate. We then begin to uncover how God is speaking to us through those thoughts. We ask, *"What are you saying to me, Father?"* We also allow God to speak a personal word to our heart.

Oratio – To Pray. Based on the way God has spoken to us through His Word and the meditations which have risen in our heart, we then respond to God's Word with the A.C.T.S. of prayer:

Adoration – Praise for who God is.
Contrition – Sorrow for sin.
Thanksgiving – Gratitude for what God has done
Supplication – Asking for the grace or blessing we need

Contemplatio – To Contemplate. We simply sit with God who has spoken to us and enjoy His presence and the way He has come to us through His Word, keeping our heart open for Him to speak even more to our spirit a personal word.

In this way, *Lectio*, we allow God to be the Lord of the Encounter and control the conversation. We also enter into a dialogue based on His word.

I suggest that you use a journal for all these steps and you literally write out all that is occurring, word for word, during your prayer time. In this way, you are praying at the point of your pen. You will be amazed at that which comes forth. Praying at the point of your pen will also help you to stay focused so that God can bring forth, with clarity, that which He longs to say to your spirit.

DAY
TeN

Day 10: Forgive Others

And when you stand praying, if you hold anything against anyone, forgive him, so that your Father in heaven may forgive you your sins. Mark 11:25

MEDITATION

It was a Tuesday night on June 21st, 1998, when it began. I was 25 years old. In the PBS series, Power of Myth, Bill Moyer interviewed the "mythologist," Joseph Campbell. I was glued to the TV for the next five weeks. I loved learning about myths and religions as they go to the core of why people do what they do as the framework of their life.

One night in the series, Bill Moyer asked the question as to what made Jesus so much different than the other "myths" of the world. Now, the answer is much more than Joseph Campbell shared. Basically, in Jesus, God became man, died to atone for mankind's sins, and rose, victorious from the dead. This is truly what separates Jesus from all other imaginations and projections of man upon the gods. There is a heresy, false teaching, that all religions are basically the same. This heresy is called syncretism. There is one who stands in the midst of all and rises to be the only Truth. It is the truth of Jesus. Even though this is the case, I did take to myself the answer that Joseph Campbell gave. I cannot quote it exactly, but it is basically that Jesus' teaching on forgiveness is radically set apart from all the other myths and religions of the world. I heard this and decided that though I knew there was more to Jesus than was presented, I would discover this one thing which, before the eyes of the mystic, prophet, guru, or enlightened one, made him different. I would understand and practice forgiveness.

For me, an old translation of the Our Father, which I saw as a kid, unlocked my understanding of this command of Jesus. I remember, at someone's house where we visited when I was pre-10 years old, there hung a piece of wood which was cut diagonally and burned into it was the Our Father. It read differently from what I learned as I grew up in a Catholic family that might not have gone to Mass every Sunday, but always prayed the basic prayers. I recall standing there wondering why it read,

"forgive us our debts as we forgive our debtors."

I had learned, as probably you had, "forgive us our trespasses as we forgive those who trespass against us."

As I explored growing in forgiveness, those words burnt on wood became my key to the way of Jesus. At 25 years old, I understood the word "debt" more than the word "trespasses". A few years before, I had received a credit card and was like a kid in the candy shop and I might have even used it in a candy shop. I had racked up around $2,500.00 and was watching the bill not getting paid down because I could only make the minimal payments and interest was having its reign. How nice it would have been to have my ledger wiped clean. If the banker could do this for me, the heavens would break open and salvation would have invaded the earth. When it comes down to it, I would not have been concerned if the bank felt excited about the cancellation of what I owed or not. I just needed them to decide to clean my slate. Feelings had nothing to do with it. What I needed was a decision for a zero-dollar balance.

Then I awoke from this wishful thinking. Though this might have been a fantasy, what is contained within it is the truth regarding forgiveness. Forgiveness, because it is part of love, is a decision and not based on feeling. Forgiveness does not deny that a hurt occurred and pretend as if nothing happened. Forgiveness acknowledges the hurt and presses through to be free of its debilitation. Here are the steps to forgiveness:

1) To forgive, one must first acknowledge that he has entered into judgement against another and found the other owing him for something the other did to cause hurt. The judgement must be recognized as a fact by the offended. Whether the offender knowingly or unknowingly committed the offense does not matter. Judgement of guilt and the need for payment to balance the scales of justice has been rendered by the offended. Also, it does not matter whether the offended has a legitimate case or not does not have a legitimate case against the offender, because it is a matter of the heart. Judgement of debt has been made and sentence for payment has been passed, in whatever amount or manner the offended needs it from the offender. By the way, all of this could be happening in the deep recess of the soul and the offended may not be aware of becoming both judge and jury.

2) Given the reality of the debt, the offended is then faced with a decision: continue in judgement with the demand of payment or make the decision, as an act of the will, not based on feelings, like the banker, to cancel the debt. The offended will not hope for or extract payment from the offender now or in the future, especially at the Last Judgement.

3) Lord Jesus also tells us to do something for our offender, our enemy. We are to:

a. Do good to them. This is the immediate action we are to take. Right when we have been hurt we should allow our hearts to search for something good we can do for the person who perpetrated the hurt, the person who is our debtor.
b. Bless them. Ask heaven to bring even more good into their life. Give them the very blessings your Father has given to you.
c. Pray and for them. Continue to hold them in your heart before the Lord.

Let us contrast these three Jesus responses with those who owe us debt to the actions of the flesh, the fallen, or carnal nature:

a. Look for an opportunity to get even and do evil to them, offend them as they have offended you.
b. Curse your enemy, your debtor, wishing them harm.
c. Let your judgmental thoughts of them continue to play out in the Court Room of your mind, justifying yourself and condemning them.

Jesus instructs us in his *School of Prayer* that the choice and action of forgiveness is a step we must take before we stand in the presence of our Father in prayer. Hear that this is a condition, a necessity, when we begin to pray. I have always found it curious, considering Jesus' teaching on prayer, that we instruct souls in the importance of daily repentance for one's sins, yet we do not teach the importance of practicing daily forgiveness. I was taught to end my day with an examination of conscience, allowing my heart to reveal any sin which I had committed during that day so that I might repent and be forgiven. Since my first days of coming to Jesus, as a teenager, I found it awfully self-centered to daily ask God to forgive me and not daily extend that same forgiveness to those who hurt me. Just from praying the *Our Father,* I knew that I had to include forgiveness in my daily prayer.

Disciple of Jesus, see your Master and Teacher pinned to the cross. His first words as he comes to the climax of his pain-wracked torture:

"Father, forgive them for they know not what they do."

As the greatest sin, the greatest offense, the costliest debt against God that has ever been committed or ever will be committed, the killing of God, *deicide*, God the Son cries out with his precious, limited breath,

"Father, forgive them for they know not what they do."

From the pulpit of the cross the Sun of Justice, the High Priest of a Better Covenant practices what he preaches. He cancelled the debt that humanity owed him. Wait, no, there is more. He cancelled the debt that you owed him because of your sin. If he has done so for us, how could we not do so for others? We must forgive, so we can be forgiven.

O, Disciple of Jesus, let the time between the offense committed against you and the time of your forgiveness become shortened. Forgive all offenses that are marked in your ledger, washing them away today, so that there is nothing to be seen. In this way, Soul of Infinite Worth, you will be like your Father in Heaven who is merciful to all.

PRAYER

Father of mercy, *Abba* of all forgiveness,
you have looked kindly upon me and forgiven all my sin, all my offenses.
It is my will and desire to forgive all who are in debt to me because of their offense, whether what they have done is known by them or unknown by them; whether I have been right in my judgement or wrong.
Holy Spirit,
Teach me to pray.
Help me to be merciful even as I have been shown mercy.
Give me the grace to practice forgiveness as part of my daily prayer.
In Jesus' name.
Amen

ACTION

- Begin to include in your night prayer before you go to bed a review of the day to see if there is anyone you need to forgive.
- With whom and what will you share from today's lesson?

REFLECTION QUESTIONS

What are some of the major times in your life that you have been forgiven by God or others?

Is there anyone in your life that you need to forgive?

What is the hardest part for you to be able to forgive?

What could you do to remind yourself make forgiveness part of your daily prayer routine?

FURTHER READING

Matthew 6:12

Romans 12:17-21

Colossians 3:13

Luke 6:27-36

Ephesians 4:31-32

1 Peter 3:9

Luke 23:34

DAY
ELEVEN

Day 11: Personal and Hidden

But when you pray, go into your room, close the door and pray to your Father, who is unseen. Then your Father, who sees what is done in secret, will reward you. Matthew 6:6

MEDITATION

As soon as I came to Jesus, which was in my teen years, being alone with the Alone was part of my prayer life. I was blessed to grow up in Arizona, in a less populated area, right on the edge of the desert. Weekends would find me by myself, wandering the Superstition and Usury Mountains. My day would be spent in the middle of nowhere, not meeting one soul. But I was not alone. I was hidden in the heart of my Father. The desert mountains of Arizona are rugged. One can wander over one ridge to the next, lost in an endless maze of canyons, whose cliffs are brown, red and purple. The beauty and the grandeur are spectacular. In the midst of this oasis of stone, I was with Him. I would read the Word, hike and contemplate that which I read. I would sit on the edge of a cliff and my heart would overflow in song, filling the valley below with my love for Him. Was I on the mountain or in Him? I would be swept away into His presence and the hours would pass without notice or care.

The Greek philosopher Aristotle, who still affects our thinking to this day, taught the Four Transcendentals. These were the attributes that pull one out of himself, transcending self to be bare before the Mystery. Beauty is one of the transcendentals, along with truth, unity and goodness. I was in the midst of beauty and I could not hold myself within, not able to resist its lure. The Navajo Indians of Arizona begin their day with this prayer, facing the sun as it rises:

In beauty, I walk.
With beauty before me I walk.
With beauty behind me I walk.
With beauty around me I walk.
With beauty above me I walk.
With beauty below me I walk.
We begin now in beauty.

This prayer is what I was experiencing and the beauty I saw drew me to God, who, himself, is beauty. There were times that the beauty of his presence was so overwhelming that I felt as if he and I were one. I felt permeable, with Him flowing into me and me flowing into Him.

Peace, quiet, being alone was one of the greatest classrooms in which Jesus instructed me in his *School of Prayer*. Not much was said by either him or me, but much was communicated by both of us to each other. These mountains were my "room" in which the lesson of Day 2, *"prayer is not what you do. It is who you are with"*, was practiced while the sun was setting and the Morning Dove was cooing.

If a soul came to me and asked how it could quickly grow in its relationship with *Hakkadosh*, the Holy One, I would invite that soul to times of solitude.

For most, entering into a time of doing nothing, but just being with the silence of the Other, is a difficult undertaking. Our senses are so overloaded that the stillness can stir the waters within which the noise of our technology keeps at bay. It is to this place you must go, O disciple of Jesus, to find him who is searching for you. It must be remembered, though, the places of exterior peace are there to train one to enter interior peace, which one carries at all times, in the sanctuary of one's heart.

For many, the desert or the forest is not within reach, given time or distance. But the knob to the radio is within reach or the remote for the TV can be put down, earbuds can be removed and the tablet can be set aside. The poisoning of Facebook is the illusion that everyone cares about everything I am doing and I need to know what others are about during their day. This gives a false sense of friendship and develops an over developed sense of self-importance. To grow in the spiritual life, one must turn things off and put them down so that silence can become the space to hear God's voice and hear one's unfiltered thoughts. Both are necessary for maturity. Give me a soul that will not embrace quiet and I will show you a soul that will be impeded in his maturity and in the depth of relationships. The soul that is full can never be emptied, to be filled with that which is lasting and satisfying.

Here, an important point of distinction should be made between the Christian mystical tradition and the other mystical ways of the world. In many a tradition, one becomes empty to be empty, one becomes quiet to be quiet. This is not the way of Jesus. The Christian becomes empty to be filled, filled with the person of God; one becomes quiet to hear, to hear the voice of God. The path of Jesus brings eternal peace because it introduces and sustains a relationship with a person who is the Prince of Peace. The other paths are paths of pseudo-peace, they offer nothing. I know this is a bold statement, but I must make it. The believer is not seeking nothing. The believer is seeking Someone because that Someone is seeking him.

Do not be tricked by false ideas that claim to lead you to be who you were created to be. We are called to encounter, not to nihilism.

What is one to do whose world does not include natural beauty and quiet within his reach? There is going to a church or one's bedroom or yard; there is the park or the coffee shop. This I know. There is a place where your *Abba* waits to be alone with you every day. It might be your favorite chair or it might be an Adoration Chapel. Find that place, find that time, and go there often to be with him who longs to be with you. Hide yourself in him.

For me, one of the given places in the desert where I would encounter our Father was in a cave. There I would light my candle and incense and sit, with the Word and my journal open, before an icon of *Jesus, the Teacher.* In that cave, I would meet the *Ancient of Days* whose days were spent watching for me to pierce the dark of the cave with my steps. You might not have a cave in the desert where you can go, but you have the cave of your heart where you can, and must, enter often to find him sitting in still expectation of your arrival.

O disciple, do not put off to tomorrow your time of hiddenness when He waits for you, today. Find your place with him and go there.

ACTION

- How much time do you spend connecting to social media? For the next week, make a record in your journal when and how long you use social media. Ask the Holy Spirit if this is weakening your spiritual life.
- With whom and what will you share from today's lesson?

REFLECTION QUESTIONS

Where are the places where you have been able to be alone with Him?

Can you recall a time or times when you encountered beauty, truth, unity, or goodness and sensed or were drawn to the presence of God?

What are some things that try to pull you away when you go to pray and how can you curb their call during that time?

Make a list of places you can go to be with the Alone:

FURTHER READING

Hosea 2:14

Luke 5:16

Mark 1:35

Exodus 3:1-6

DAY

Twelve

Day 12: Personal, but not Private

"Again, I tell you that if two of you on earth agree about anything you ask for, it will be done for you by my Father in heaven. For where two or three come together in my name, there am I with them." Matthew 18:19-20

MEDITATION

I waited and waited for the day to come. Over three hundred had gathered. The music was phenomenal. My best friend had also come to share the moment. Two of my other best friends were there, one ready to give the blessing and the other with a message to point the way. When she entered the room, tears began to fill my eyes and my best friend jabbed me in the side so as to say, "Toughen up!" As the perfect song played she walked toward me. There was no doubt by anyone there that she was the most beautiful girl in the room. She came to me as the greatest gift I had ever received and he was with her, he was with all of us. It was he that was worshipping his Father, our Father, through, with, and in us and we who were worshipping the Father through, with, and in him. The day had come and it was when Andrea and I were joined together to Jesus at our wedding.

In *Jesus' School of Prayer,* it is important that we enter into a personal relationship with Jesus. It is a powerful moment when a seeker comes to believe that Jesus died personally for him, on the cross, and not just for all of creation, and now that believer knows that whenever he prays, God, his *Abba,* his *Papa* hears and cares. We must also recognize, too, that this relationship, though personal, is not private. It is twisted to believe in *"Me and Jesus"* and not include *"We and Jesus."* Jesus has made us his body. We are individual members that are connected together. We are the Household of Faith, the Family of God, the Church. There was never a belief in the whole of the Christian experience until recently that one could be a Christian, but not connected to the Church. This is just a fallacy. It is wrong and contrary to the whole of the Biblical experience of God as recorded through the Old and New Testament as well as the lives of the redeemed throughout the centuries.

Liturgical prayer is central and essential to *Jesus' School of Prayer.* Liturgical prayer is when Jesus, through the ritual prayer of his body which has been passed down since the founding of his Church, worships the Father on earth as is in heaven. Liturgical prayer mirrors on earth all that is occurring in the Temple of Heaven, right now, as Jesus, the High Priest, leads all to fall down before the Throne. It is not the invention of great men with pious thoughts as to how worship would best suit the people. Though the people are an important consideration for a Bible study, in liturgy the needs of the people are not the focus. Liturgy is the action of Jesus and those invited to the Wedding of the Lamb uniting together as one for the praise of the Father and the salvation of the world. Liturgy is not a mere human event. It is the event of the God-Man, Jesus, where he re-members all to his saving death and resurrection. Liturgy, the Mass, is the highest expression of *"two or three gathering together in his name"* and he in their midst. No occasion in human history is comparable. It is the one assembly that is like no other of this earth.

It is at the liturgy, the Mass, that the New Covenant is celebrated and made present. It is in those eternal moments when the sons and daughters of God may eat the flesh of their Christ and become one with him. Their communion is with the total Christ who is incarnate and risen, who is consumed both spiritually and physically. As with the marital covenant, the two become one in every aspect of being because he who is the Word said,

"This is my body. This is my blood of the new covenant. Take and eat."

In the eating, those who partake become what they eat; they become *flesh of his flesh and bone of his bone*. The two are co-mingled with us abiding in him and he is abiding in us. Holy Communion, the Eucharist, is a pinnacle moment when we are gathered in his name and he is truly and completely in our midst.

O disciple of Jesus, you are invited to the Mystery of mysteries. How could you refrain from the most precious moment of encounter in which you will ever stand? At every Mass, he waits for you so that together you may worship the Father in Spirit and in truth.

PRAYER

Abba, Father,
through, with and in Jesus, by the power of the Holy Spirit, may all glory and honor be yours forever.
I stand in awe that I have become one with your son, Jesus, through his selfless sacrifice of Calvary where he has given me all that he is and has.
Holy Spirit,
teach me to pray.
Jesus,

thank you for the gift of the Mass when we gather and you are truly present.

Cause me to long for its next celebration and draw my heart deeper and deeper into the mystery in which I stand of the two becoming one, though they are many.

Father, my *Papa*,

I pray this in Jesus' name.

Amen

ACTION

- The next time you are together with other believers, become aware of Jesus being in your midst.
- With whom and what will you share from today's lesson?

REFLECTION QUESTIONS

Do you have a moment when you sensed the presence of Jesus when you were gathering with other believers?

As you read the MEDITATION, what most drew you into thought?

How would you describe your relationship with Jesus, your Eucharistic Lord?

How would you tell someone else about the importance of liturgical prayer?

FURTHER READING

Acts 2:42

1 John 1:7

Psalm 133:1

Hebrews 10:25

1 Corinthians 12:12-27

Day 13: In the Spirit

"Yet a time is coming and has now come when the true worshipers will worship the Father in spirit and truth, for they are the kind of worshipers the Father seeks. God is spirit, and his worshipers must worship in spirit and in truth." John 4:23-24

MEDITATION

I pray that today's lesson in the *Disciple's School of Prayer* is not too esoteric. I want it to be practical and applicable. You might need to read it over and over to digest its truths since you probably are not used to thinking about this subject.

There is so much buried treasure for us in the story of our father and mother, Adam and Eve. One of the most important truths is who they were before the fall to the first sin, what changed in them because of the fall, and what Jesus has done to restore in us what was lost with the fall.

In scripture we learn, over and over, that man is an integrated composite of body, soul, and, spirit. In understanding the function of the body, soul, and spirit, as well as the order of supremacy of the three, we can better understand the work of the spiritual life.

When I ask people, *"Who created you?"*, the overwhelming response is God. Wait, I am a parent of ten. I think my wife and I, also, had something to do with the creation of our children. At the moment of conception, the Father creates the spirit of each person while the parents contribute the matter for the physical body. Man is both material and immaterial. Imagine two circles, one circle is the spirit and the other circle is the body. Now, see these two circles slightly overlapping. The space that is created from the overlap of the circles is the soul. The soul is a combination of one's spirit and body.

Now, let's precisely define the function of each of the components of our person:

Body – Systems and senses
Soul – Mind, will, and emotions
Spirit – Communion with and revelation from God

Before the fall, man was governed toward things above by his spirit being in communion with the Holy Spirit, by which he received revelation. This revelation informed his soul (mind, will, and emotions) to decide and desire rightly to employ his body (system and senses) in service of the revelation he received. This is known as the spiritual man, the man who is controlled by his spirit in the Holy Spirit. The spiritual man's heart is set on things above. The cry of the spiritual man's soul is *"Thy will be done."* The spiritual man lives for the Trinity and in his living, offers worship to the Holy Trinity. The focus of the life of the spiritual man is the emptying of self for the other, trusting to be filled from the infinite life of God, Himself, who is a Giver and rushes to flood and take care of those who give. The spiritual man finds joy in giving because he knows that he draws from an unlimited source and with this in mind, there is no need to form attachments. The spiritual man lives under the Law of Abundance.

After the fall, man's body (system and senses) and/or soul (mind, will, and emotions) governed his body and he was pulled to things below. This man is known as the carnal man or the fallen man. The cry of the carnal man's soul is, *"I want what I want and I want it now."* The carnal man worships the unholy trinity of me, myself, and I. Even the giving of the carnal man is self-centered, bringing glory to self. The carnal man is seeking to receive and when emptying himself must fill himself, since he, in the end, is all he has, and what he has is limited and finite. When the carnal man turns to others to fill him he draws from them what is limited and finite, leaving him wanting. This want then, can leave him to grab and hoard. The carnal man is ruled by the Law of Scarcity.

Jesus has sanctified us by restoring the order to that of the spiritual man. We, those who are hungering for holiness, are living in communion with the Holy Spirit who reveals to us the Father's will and we correctly reason, choose, and desire to do the will of the Father with our bodies.

With this model in mind, becoming more spiritual is not attained by self-will or will power. Christianity is not the *"try harder religion"* or *"the ultimate self-improvement course."* True Christianity is surrender to the Sanctifier, the Holy Spirit, for him to do his work in us and through us. For the spiritual believer, growth and maturity in Christ is from our spirit being in communion with the Holy Spirit, and as we abide in Jesus, we will produce the fruit of righteousness.

Our soul is the fulcrum, tipping point, for us to choose the things that are above or the things that are below. When we come to our final breath, either our soul and body will be pulled up and identified with our spirit or our spirit will have been captured and ensnared by our soul and our body. The soul that is identified with the spirit will go off to heaven to await the resurrection of the body unto righteousness, while the spirit that is

66

ensnared by the soul and body will resurrect unto damnation. In the end, we will simply pursue the treasure that has won our heart.

Our prayer life, then, is about growing into deeper communion with the Holy Spirit so that he might grant us revelation as to how to live in each moment to do the will of our Father. This is the dialogue of prayer which spills into the practicality of daily life.

In *Jesus' School of Prayer,* we are to worship in spirit and in truth. The spirit of which Jesus is speaking is not the Holy Spirit *(note that spirit is not capitalized),* but our spirit. Because the saving grace of Jesus has been poured into us through the waters of Baptism our spirit has come alive and is indwelt with the Holy Spirit. We have been born again, meaning that our spirit, which was dead because of original sin, has now been made alive in Jesus. The spiritual life is about keeping the right order of surrendering to the Holy Spirit to fill our spirit so as to grant revelation to our soul that we might rightly use our body.

There are three stages to prayer in the spiritual life:

Discursive – One speaking to God (Body)
Meditative – One's mind dwelling on the things of God. (Soul)
Contemplative – One living in union with God where God speaks to
        him. (Spirit)

The contemplative stage is the highest of the three and it employs the other two. Our spirit living in the Holy Spirit is the contemplative stage. With this in mind, our prayer time needs to be, above all, a time of sitting with the Lord, trusting and allowing him to write upon our souls. You might ask how this is done. How does one get a sun tan? They place themselves in the sun, surrendering to the work of its rays, knowing and trusting that the sun will do its job and our skin will tan. This is the contemplative way, and now you also know it as the way of the spiritual man. We place ourselves before the Lord Jesus, in total abandonment, and trust that the Holy Spirit will transform us into his likeness.

Lastly, I want to mention the use of our soul and body in prayer. Sometimes the ways of the soul, especially the emotions, are downplayed or disdained. This is unfortunate since the Father created our soul and loves it. He must have a plan for our soul and our body in His redemption. It is this: our soul and body must be submitted to our spirit and not rule over our spirit. When the soul is surrendered to the Holy Spirit, the Spirit will use the emotions in their right order and will use the body in its right order. When we pray and worship the Lord, we decide to use the emotions to draw us into deeper, heartfelt devotion to the Lord. The body should also be engaged in prayer so that the whole person is worshipping God.

This is why we make the sign of the cross, lift or fold our hands, kneel or lay prostrate, when we pray. In doing these things we are praying with our body.

PRAYER

Father, my *Daddy*,
I am fearfully and wonderfully made – spirit, soul, and body.
I offer all that I am as a living sacrifice to you.
I am completely and totally yours.
Sanctify me body, soul, and spirit.
Holy Spirit,
teach me to pray.
Fill me with your presence.
I want to live in communion with you and receive your revelation to be able to live my life in your will.
In Jesus' name.
Amen

ACTION

- Spend some time sitting before the Lord today before you make a decision, and allow Him to speak as to His will.
- With whom and what will you share from today's lesson?

REFLECTION QUESTIONS

What insight did you receive from this lesson?

If you were to explain this MEDITATION to someone, what would you say? Which form of prayer, discursive, meditative or contemplative, do you find yourself using most often?

In what ways are you walking as the spiritual man?

In what way does the carnal man take over in your life?

FURTHER READING

1 Thessalonians 5:23

Colossians 3:1-3

John 15:5

Matthew 6:21

2 Corinthians 3:17-18

PRAYER HELP: Casual & Passionate Presence

I must admit that it is wonderfully amazing when you experience the tangible presence of God, either in your spirit or in your body.

Day 14: Father Gives Good Gifts

Which of you, if his son asks for bread, will give him a stone? Or if he asks for a fish, will give him a snake? If you, then, though you are evil, know how to give good gifts to your children, how much more will your Father in heaven give good gifts to those who ask him! Matthew 7:9-11

MEDITATION

I was not blessed to grow up with a dad, so when I came to Jesus, one of the first things he did was introduce me to his Father and leave me, for years, with his Father. We are called to have a personal relationship with each member of the Trinity, but my relationship with Jesus and the Holy Spirit did not develop for at least 20 some years after I surrendered my life to Jesus' Lordship. Since Jesus led me to the Father, I only know the Father that Jesus knows. I have never known the false god who is waiting to send people to hell. I have never known the false god who stands against me and withholds his presence and blessing. I have only known the Father as Jesus knows the Father – kind and gentle, meek and humble of heart. My moments with Him, my AhDah, are times of being lost in His love and affirmation, His encouragement and His guidance. I have only known my AhDah to be a good Father. I know that Jesus did this for me to heal the wounds caused by the absence of my earthly dad, God rest his soul.

I prophesy and believe that the next move of God, of which we are in the beginnings, is the Movement of the Fatherhood of God. We have seen the Jesus Movement which led souls into a personal, radical, life-transforming encounter with Jesus Christ. Then we saw the great outpouring of the Holy Spirit through the Charismatic Renewal where soul upon soul experienced the Baptism of the Holy Spirit and began to move in the power of God through the gifts of the Spirit.

Now is the time for believers to know their Father as their Abba, their Daddy, their Papa, and experience the Father's Baptism of Love. These Baptized in the Father's Love souls, beloved sons and daughters with whom the Father is well pleased, will go forth into a sin-sick, dark, world, not with judgment and wrath, but with the Father's presence and power to display His mercy and goodness. Disciple of Jesus, long to be one of these souls. Give your Father permission to be your Abba and baptize you in His love and then take to others His mercy and goodness.

To enter into this Baptism of Love, one of the issues which needs to be settled in every heart that learns from the *School of Prayer* is that of the goodness of God. The question is: Do you believe that God will always be good to you in all situations? Or, do you fear that if you walk in His will you could be hurt by Him?

A great lie of the enemy is to get us to doubt the goodness of God. This is how the liar came to me. I was going through the most difficult time I had ever faced in my life. Much was taken from me and in the eyes of the world I should have sued to bring justice. I lost my livelihood and much of all that I possessed. I also lost my reputation before people who did not know the complete story and should have known the story. Lawyers told me that I had a good lawsuit which would leave me set for the rest of my life. I chose the path of forgiveness and to trust my needs and my future to my AhDah, my Father.

In the midst of the hurt, given I was betrayed by people I trusted, I was going to counseling to protect and heal my broken heart. Yes, I must admit, there were times of anger which rose in my heart. As the counselor was working with me, she once said, "Brendan, we have worked through many of the situations where you were gravely hurt. I know you are a devout man. I think it is time to address the anger you might have toward God."

I quickly retorted, "How can I be angry with the very one who wants to help and heal me in the midst of all this pain and anger? He did not do this to me, so why would I be angry with Him?"

One of the most debilitating acts of the enemy is to get you to question the goodness of God toward you. When something painful happens in our life the enemy is right there to say, "Where is your God?" In this he is trying to get us to turn from the very one who did not cause our pain; He is, though, the one who is with us and ready to help us in our pain.

What I am about to say is very strong. After hearing it, please pray and ask the Holy Spirit if it is true. Pop spirituality and pop psychology would encourage us to embrace any anger we might have toward God and express it. To this, I offer a question: Who would have us get angry with God? The Holy Spirit or the evil spirit? Of course, it is the evil spirit who would inspire us to get angry with God, our loving and caring Father. We have no right to become angry with God. If you have become angry with God I invite you to repent, to acknowledge that you were wrong, and ask his forgiveness, so that nothing will stand in the way of your relationship with Him or block the blessings He longs to give you.

Disciple, make this stance in your heart, right now. Your Father will only give you good gifts. He will never do anything to harm you. Your Abba will not give you a stone when you need bread and your Papa will not give you a snake when you need fish. He is a good Father who only does good to His children. Many times, I think we try to protect God by saying that He must not have willed the good thing for which we were asking because He was concerned for our soul. Why do we not stick with the revelation of Jesus of his Father and when things do not work out as we prayed, we should return to the words of Jesus, believing God to be a good Father as we continue to pray for the breakthrough and for the good we need? I have come to the point of refusing to answer for God, even to myself. I will let Him answer for Himself on resurrection morning. Meanwhile, I will continue to take Jesus at his Word.

There will be a problem in our prayer life if we do not settle in our souls that God is a good Father and that He only does good. We will be fearful of what He really wants and will do to us. How can this soul trust Him? How can this soul abandon itself to Him when He might hurt it?

O Disciple, today, right now, choose in your heart to believe the truth, knowing that when you pray the Father is always going to give you good things.

PRAYER

Father,
I believe that you are a good Father and, therefore, I trust you.
Thank you that you will never harm me.
Thank you that you are ready to give me every good gift.
Father,
be my *Abba* and baptize me in your love and I will take your mercy and goodness to a confused world that is covered with thick darkness.
In the midst of the darkness, I will arise and shine with your glory,
Yahweh, upon me.
Holy Spirit,
teach me to pray.
Jesus,
Teach me to believe in the Father in which you believe and to stand in the confidence of a son/daughter who is loved.
In Jesus' name.
Amen

ACTION

- In your journal make a list of all the good things your Father has done for you.

73

- With whom and what will you share from today's lesson?

REFLECTION QUESTION

In what areas of your life do you find it hardest to trust God as a loving Father?

Have you ever blamed God for something painful that happened in your life?

Have you ever experienced the Father's personal love for you?

FURTHER READING

John 14:9

Psalm 119:68

James 1:17

Psalm 34:8

Psalm 23:6

Isaiah 60:1-3

Day 15: The Word as Your Home

To the Jews who had believed him, Jesus said, "If you make my word your home, you are truly my disciples." John 8:31 *(Jerusalem Bible)*

MEDITATION

Into the wall, I ran. Not only was my toe bleeding, but so was my nose. Needless to say, my wife came bolting out of bed, given the not so sweet poetry that was flowing from my mouth, wondering what had just happened. What happened is we had just been married and I was living in a new place. I grew up in my parent's home. If I woke in the middle of the night I would roll out of bed to my left, take six steps forward, turn left and take five steps and turn right, walk four more and I was there at the place we will not mention that sometimes you need to visit in the middle of the night. Here was the problem, our apartment was not my home. I did not know my way around in the dark, with my eyes barely open.

For many of a believer, this is the case when it comes to God's Word. It is not their home, so they do not know their way around, especially when they need the truth that sets one free.

The disciple of the Lord Jesus is trained to abide, to make his home, in the Word of God. This disciple knows his way around the Word and can stand on the Word's great and precious promises. When the need arises, the disciple of the Lord Jesus reaches for the Word, whether on the shelf or hidden in his heart through memorization, and stands on that Word, believing what he sees in the Word more than what he sees in his circumstances. This is the stance of faith. The decision that must be made by the believer is this – Is God's Word the truth? Once the believer settles in his heart that God's Word is the truth, then the believer moves to being a disciple, ready to be trained in the truth and live from that truth, bringing the Kingdom into the earth as it is in heaven.

It is the Word which is the basis for the disciple's prayer time, be it through discursive *(speaking, conversing)* prayer or meditation *(the heart mulling over a passage)*. This is the way of prayer preserved by the monks whose day is a rhythm of praying the Word and meditating on the Word as they work. This rhythm sanctifies time, bringing the presence of God, by praying the Word, into all they are and all they do.

Can anyone argue that this is not a powerful way to live? Imagine what your life would be like if it was injected by encounters with God, through His Word, throughout the day. This is your inheritance, O son, O daughter of God. I was blessed to be taught, right from the beginning, how to walk in the ways of the Lord, using the Word of God as the basis of my prayer time. I will never forget the Jerusalem Bible I bought when I moved from a believer to a committed disciple of the Lord, and the feeling of taking that Bible into my hand, cracking it open, knowing I was holding onto that which gives life. I was so in love that I kissed that Bible.

I try to kiss my Bible every time I open it to this day. It has become my home from which I daily live. I have grasped it to my heart, with tears, in the most difficult times and found His presence rushing to me even as I held it. I have stood before it with pages laid bare for me to place both hands on it as I rejoiced or enjoyed His sweet presence leaving it with the smell of me from the patchouli oil, which I wear. It has become my home. When the night of life has left the way to go too difficult to see, His Word has been the lamp that shows me the way, keeping me at peace, trusting in His promises as I watched those promises fulfilled. Give me a soul to form in the life of the Spirit and I will give that soul the Word of God.

As I mentioned, the Word is the basis of the disciple's prayer time, be it discursive or meditative. The psalms are a powerful way for discursive prayer. The Jews, which would include Jesus, read the psalms out loud as a part of their prayer time. To this day, the Church does the same in praying the Liturgy of the Hours. I have written a simplified version of the Hours and placed it in the back of this Manual. This version allows you to pray the Hours from your Bible. You can also buy a set of the Liturgy of the Hours. Many use a shortened form – *Magnificat* or *Give Us This Day*. I have also included in the appendix, a table to pray the psalms three times a day for 30 days, which will take you through the entire Book of Psalms.

How I pray the psalms is to use them as a spring board for my conversation with the Lord. I will read, out loud, the entire psalm, end with the *Glory Be* and then allow my heart to look back over what I read and let the words of the psalms move me into my own words. One of the beauties of praying the psalms is the variety of emotions which the psalms express. One needs to remember, as was the lesson for Day 11, that we are members of the Body of Christ. By praying the psalms, the Church teaches that we are uniting our self to Jesus as he makes this prayer through all his members. There are times when you will pray the psalms and it is giving voice to a time of great difficulty, yet your heart is rejoicing. At that time, Jesus, our High Priest, is praying through you for those in difficult situations. At other times, it is the opposite. When praying the psalms, you can also be comforted that whatever you are facing, another member of the Body of Christ, along with Jesus, is standing with you in that same circumstance.

Here is a prayer that I pray when praying the psalms from my Bible: *Father, I join myself to Jesus, as he prays these prayers through all people, through all time, in all circumstances. In Jesus' name.*

In this way, I am acting upon the priestly anointing I received at my baptism. A priest stands between God and man to offer praise and make supplication. A priest raises his hands to bless *Yahweh* and then lowers those hands to bless the people. Disciple of Jesus, you are a royal priest. May your prayer be for more than you and your concerns. May you bring all creation and all mankind with you as you stand before His throne.

The disciple's prayer, based on the Word, is also a time of meditation. After a period of discursive prayer, the disciple then turns to the Word to hear what the Spirit is saying. The Hebrew word for meditation paints the picture of a cow chewing the cud. In meditation, the disciple slowly reads the passage from the Word, three to four times, each time allowing the Word to come into the spirit to be broken down so as to pass into the soul for its nourishment. The grace of the Sacraments feeds and transforms the spirit, while the revelation of God's Word enlightens, heals, and transforms the soul so that the soul comes to the likeness of Jesus. Through meditating on the Word, the soul puts on the mind of Christ.

O disciple of Jesus, next time you come to prayer, make sure to have the Word of God with you, opening it, believing that your Father wants to speak to you. Do not wait any longer to meet your Father through His Word.

PRAYER

Father,
thank you for the gift of your Word.
Thank you that your Word is life and truth.
It is my desire that I come to find a home in it.
Holy Spirit,
teach me to pray.
Jesus,
as your disciple, teach me how to bring your Word into my daily prayer time.
Speak, Lord, your servant is listening.
In Jesus' name.
Amen

ACTION

- Whenever you read something and a Bible passage is cited, look it up in your Bible.
- With whom and what will you share from today's lesson?

REFLECTION QUESTIONS

How comfortable are you finding your way around the Bible?

What part does the Word of God play in your life?

What is a passage or passages from the Bible which really speaks to your heart?

How could you incorporate the Bible into your daily prayer time?

FURTHER READING

Psalm 1

Joshua 1:6-9

James 1:21-25

Jeremiah 15:16

Mark 4:1- 20

Day 16: Three Great Gifts

Ask and it will be given to you; seek and you will find; knock and the door will be opened to you. For everyone who asks receives; he who seeks finds; and to him who knocks, the door will be opened. Matthew 7:7-8

MEDITATION

I am so grateful that from the beginning of my relationship with Jesus Christ I have always known that he will take care of me in every way. As the years have passed, over and over I see his hand of blessing. He has not only taken care of me physically, but also emotionally, spiritually, and intellectually. Some think that he just cares about their spiritual well-being. When we look at the life of the Master we see that his love knew no bounds and he supplied for every need that he saw others facing.

In his *School of Prayer,* we are invited by him to lay everything before him in trust. His generosity says to us - ask, seek, find - and they come with the assurance that when we ask, we will receive, not might receive; when we seek, we will find; when we knock the door will be opened. Given these guarantees, with what faith-filled confidence we can proceed. So many believers are impoverished in either their bodies, souls or spirits because they see themselves with their skills and experience to be the source to supply their need. Of course, we are to put to use our skill and experience, but this is always done with the heart-truth that He is the real hand behind the provision. If believers would start with prayer instead of relying on self, how quickly heaven would come rushing to their aid. I wonder how many unclaimed blessings are piled in heaven because those predestined for blessings are never claimed?

There are three areas of entreaty in this lesson of our Lord that we are to cover in prayer. We are to ask for our body, seek for our soul, and knock for our spirit.

Ask and Receive for our Bodily Needs

Here, we are given the opportunity to lay before our generous Father our physical needs. He cares that we have the food we need and money for gas to drive to work. There is nothing for which we should not approach Him to take care of our bodies. We should expose all our life to Him with great trust in His Fatherly love. When we need a car, to Him we should turn. When our children need braces, to Him we should turn. When we need healing, before we see the doctor we should see our *Abba*. When an unexpected bill arrives in our mail, to Him we should turn. We should do the same with every expected bill, even when we have the money to pay it, immediately. By turning to Him in times of abundance and time of need we are training our hearts to realize two things: 1) all belongs to Him and is to be used for Him and 2) what we have has come from Him and should remind us that we always need Him.

We should also become aware in our turning to Him that He wants us to be a blessing to others and take care of their needs. We are to excel in our giving. Pray that he sends to you those in need, for this is a great honor and blessing to share from what you have been given. Never see the person in need, especially the poor, as a burden; see them, rather, as a blessing in their outstretched hands. Be grateful that the one in need has approached you. In your giving, yes, be wise, but never let your heart be ensnared by the lie of the Law of Scarcity. God is your Father and we live under the *Law of Abundance*.

Seek and Find for the Needs of Our Soul

Know that Jesus stands ready to give to you all you are seeking for your soul (intellect, will, and emotions). He is ready to strengthen your will, to fortify you with the power you need to resist every onslaught of the evil one. You are not powerless if you pray. You are not a victim. You are an overcomer. You are not weak. You are strong. All he has is at your disposal.

Jesus even cares about your "smarts". He loves your ability to reason and your ability to remember. Your brain is the most complex piece of creation in the entire universe and every time you use it, be it in the loftiest way or in the simplest way, He receives glory. He has given you this gift and He wants to be included in its care and increase. Seek for an increase of your intellect. It glorifies Him when you read a book and discover a new truth. It glorifies Him when you watch another and their skill becomes yours.

He is not only the healer of bodies, but also of our hearts, our emotions and memories. Seek Jesus to heal the brokenness of your heart. Life can wound us and we seem to believe that in forgetting, all will be well. The majority of times we react to situations because of what has happened to us in the past. Jesus, the healer of all, is ready to reach into the long forgotten, dark depths of our past and bring his light and truth to set us free. How few avail themselves of Jesus and all he desires to do for them to set them free so that their past does not equal their present or future. What a sad condition when believers are trapped and shackled by their past manifesting in the present circumstance, destructive behavior and thoughts. Jesus stands before them with the key of release.

Knock and It is Opened for Our Spirit

Jesus wants there to be nothing hidden from you regarding the ways of his Kingdom to be enacted in every situation in your life, whether it be the need for the revelation of truth or for power and authority. He wants you to read his Word and for his Word to speak into your life. When you take up the Word, knock and the door of understanding will be opened to you. Do not approach his Word as any ordinary book that you take in hand. Set about his Word, knowing that its author, the Holy Spirit, dwells within you and is ready to teach. Nothing else that has ever been written in human history, when read, brings the author to live within the one who is reading, who then instructs that reader in what the Author has written. The Holy Spirit is your teacher. Knock and he will come, ready to reveal to you what is hidden to the carnal mind. How blessed we are to have been given the gift of the Holy Spirit. Our Father not only gives us commands through the Spirit, he instructs us in those commands, and by the Spirit, he empowers us to live the commands that he has given.

We are also to knock on the Door of the Graces of Authority to open to us. It is for us to advance His Kingdom and drive out every work of darkness. There is no need for us to fear the enemy and his tactics. We have the authority and the power to cast him out and down to the fiery pit. We are the sons and daughters of God, appointed and anointed to be about our Father's business.

When the Door of Authority is entered by a believer, through this door he finds what is needed to help a hurting world. Signs and wonders, healing, prophetic utterance, the power to set the captive free, and even the authority to control nature are made available to those who knock with faith.

In the *School of Prayer*, Jesus is clear that if you ask you will receive. He is clear that if you seek you will find. And, he is clear that if you knock it shall be opened to you. There is no need to doubt, O disciple, your teacher is telling you to approach the Father's throne of grace for everything. Do not delay allowing your Father to give you all.

PRAYER

Father, my *Papa*,
there is no area of my life from which your hand of providence does not want to touch with blessing.
From now on I will ask knowing that I will receive.

From now on I will seek knowing that I will find.
From now on I will knock knowing that it will be opened to me.
Holy Spirit,
teach me to pray.
Jesus,
I am ready to receive all that you have for me.
I do not want to there to be any unclaimed blessings or graces which you
have for me.
I receive them all and will turn to you for all.
In Jesus' name.
Amen

ACTION

- Spend some time reviewing your life and make a list in your
  journal of what you need for your body, soul, and your spirit.
- With whom and what will you share from today's lesson?

REFLECTION QUESTIONS

What insights did you draw from this lesson?

Given what Jesus has taught, how should you be changing in your life to
receive all that he has for you?

In what area of your life do you think there are unclaimed blessings or
graces because you have not turned to him?

Before you pay a bill, what could you do to remind yourself that all has
come from Him and to be used for Him?

84

FURTHER READING

Ephesians 1:17

2 Corinthians 9:10

Luke 10:19

Ephesians 3:20

DAY

Seventeen

Day 17: Tell Him Your Heart's Desire

"What do you want me to do for you?" Jesus *asked him.* Mark 10:51

MEDITATION

The other day, I was sitting in my chair and my two-year-old son, Jonathan, came to me with great concern in his eyes. The bucket for his John Deere toy tractor was broken off. He mumbled away words that I did not understand and his hands gestured in frustration. I was caught up in watching him express his concern and his confidence that I could help him. For him, that tractor was the need that must be addressed at the moment before anything else was done and I was the solution.

On two levels, I find it interesting that Jesus asks what he can do for us. First, should we be asking him what we can do for him? He is the Lord of the Universe to whom every knee shall bend, yet, with this question, he is speaking as a servant. *"What can I do for you?"* should be the question which I am asking of him. Secondly, the man to whom Jesus addresses this question is a blind man. Why would Jesus ask a blind man what he wanted? Is it not obvious? Here is the truth – Jesus loves us and does not presume our need. In this way, he is not forcing himself on us, though his love wants to take care of all that we need. So, Jesus will inquire of what we see as our need. There is a deep respect in Jesus for us and what we see as our need.

In his bestselling book, **The Five Languages of Love**, Gary Chapman has identified that there are five ways in which a person expresses and desires to be loved. Spirituality is at its essence our experience of God and the expression of our relationship with Him. Therefore, truths of human relationships are truths we can apply to our relationship with God. I believe that these *Five Languages* are also ways in which we express our love to God and we need God to express His love to us. In the *School of Prayer,* I think it is important to recognize the way we want our *Daddy* to demonstrate His love for us and for us to identify the way in which we would naturally express love to Him. In defining our love language, we then will be able to answer the question of Jesus, "*What do you want me to do for you?*"

The Five Languages of Love are these: Gift Giving, Quality Time, Words of Affirmation, Acts of Service and Physical Touch.

Gift Giving – Those whose love language is gift giving primarily feel blessed when their Father meets their material needs. In prayer, they make known the material desires of their heart. This is not greed. We are all in material need. It is a problem when one becomes greedy or covetous. If this is not the case, the person whose language is gift giving should lay their desires before the Father. The believers who find this to be their love language are called to be givers to others so that our generous and kind Father might use them to express his love in taking care of others.

Quality Time – People whose love language is quality time enjoy long periods of prayer, drawing near to the Lord as the Lord draws near to them. They are drawn to Eucharistic Adoration and quiet time. These believers long to spend time with the Lord. These souls know that the members of the Trinity are always ready to spend time with those who make themselves available. Those who are blessed to have quality time as their love language are the available presence of the Father to those who need the close company of someone to walk with them through life

Words of Affirmation – The believer who yearns for words of affirmation in their relationship with God are those who read the Word of God to hear the Father's life-giving Word to them. These hearts are attracted to listening in their time of prayer knowing that their Father will speak words of encouragement and comfort. The Holy Spirit expresses himself through these believers by building up others through the same words of encouragement and comfort which they have received.

Acts of Service – Those whose love language is acts of service experience the love of God when God comes to their aid. These souls experience His love when they are facing a problem and the Lord brings them relief or a solution. Believers whose love language is acts of service best loves God by laying down their life in service of others.

Physical Touch - The language of the love of God for some is that of physical touch. These souls realize that they have more senses than just the physical ones, they know that their spirit also has senses. At times, God's love pours out on these sons and daughters with a heightened awareness of the Father's presence lovingly surrounding them. These believers are the ones who are always willing to hug and embrace, they are there to give a pat on the back to someone who has done a great work for the Lord or others.

None of these languages is higher than the other. Different souls need different expressions. Unfortunately, in the spiritual life, we tend to promote one love language over another and because of this a soul that does not have that love language becomes discouraged and not drawn to a deep, intimate relationship with the Lord.

PRAYER

Father,
whose heart is filled with love for me, thank you for your willingness to express your love for me in the language which speaks to my soul.
Jesus,
What do I want?
I want to be loved.
Holy Spirit,
teach me to pray.
Help me to express my love for the Father and others in the way in which I was made to love.
I love you Lord and I open my heart to experience more of your love.
In Jesus' name.
Amen

ACTION

- Ask the Holy Spirit to show you which is the love language that you speak and then ask your *Abba,* your *Daddy,* your *Papa* to love you in that way.
- With whom and what will you share from today's lesson?

REFLECTION QUESTIONS

What is your primary love language?

What difference will knowing your love language make in your relationship with the Father?

Knowing your love language, how can you be an expression of the Father's love to others?

How is the Father making His love known to you through the other love languages?

FURTHER READING

Matthew 6:25-34

Exodus 33:12-16

Mark 1:9-11

John 13:1-17

Psalm 34:8

Day 18: Believe to Receive

Therefore, I tell you, whatever you ask for in prayer, believe that you have received it, and it will be yours. Mark 11:24

MEDIATION

"This is too good to be true!" would be the proper response to what Jesus has taught in today's lesson in his *School of Prayer*. But then, again, would this not be the same appropriate comeback for all that Jesus offers us? Everything Jesus extends to us in the Kingdom is something that should cause us to stop and say, *"Wait, it can't be that good!"* If you really understand all that Jesus has supplied for you, Disciple, then all he has done and all he has given will cause you to reply with remarks of astonishment. Here are some things which should draw forth such remarks:

The Father's love is unconditional for you, meaning, no matter what you do, you will still be loved.

"This is too good to be true!"

The Father will be forever faithful towards you, even if you betray and deny Him.

"This is too good to be true!"

Your eternal life has been purchased at the price of the life of Jesus.

"This is too good to be true!"

Every spiritual blessing is yours in the heavens through Christ Jesus.

"This is too good to be true!"

Jesus rose from the dead and because he lives, someday, you will rise from the dead.

"This is too good to be true!"

If we do not remark with the same astonishment to these truths, then why do we stand in disbelief when it comes to this promise which Jesus has made in his *School of Prayer*? If you are to doubt, then doubt that your life was worth the price of his life. To me, the sweet exchange of his life for yours is more dumbfounding, scandalous, and unbelievable than this edict of the Kingdom.

The ways of the Kingdom are lavish. They are just too much because everything in the Kingdom flows from love. Love, true love, by its very nature is lavish and cannot be contained. This promise of Jesus, believe and you shall receive, is lavish and it is a declaration whose foundation is love. With this in mind, now see it again and it will be clear that it must be as he has said. Any less would betray who he is, for he is love.

What are we to believe to receive? Before we approach believing for what we have asked, we must first examine to whom it is that we have made the request. All lessons return to the first few lessons in the *School of Prayer*. We believe that the one to whom we are turning is our *Papa*, our Father, and He is a good and generous Father who is pleased to give us the Kingdom.

In this lesson, Jesus is soliciting the act of stepping into provisional faith *(believing that God will provide)* on the part of the disciple who is praying. Faith is the essence of how things move in the Kingdom of God and without faith, it is impossible to please God. But with faith, one is pleasing to God. When you turn to *Yahweh, El Shaddai,* and lay your need before Him, you are growing in faith, trusting in the providence of the goodness of the Lord. Your confident faith is a step of faith towards a deeper relationship with your *Abba* and it is a step of faith to grow in the knowledge and experience that he provides. The step also releases an expansion of faith into greater realms of trust and these realms of greater trust allow the Holy Spirit to expand the heart for even more faith, and more faith means that more of the Kingdom can invade the earth.

With this in mind, growing souls in his ways, ask "big", so in the Lord's answering, he might even receive grander glory. The Saints were brave and they placed upon the Lord requests that only He could fulfill. And in this way, only he could receive praise and glory in the answering. When you ask, make your appeal known with great confidence, based on the words of Jesus, that your appeal will be answered, believing to receive, in the manner in which you have asked. Resist the lies and deceptions of the flesh which would seduce you away from remaining in agreement with what he has taught.

How much of the Kingdom is not breaking forth into the earth, but restrained in the heavens, because of souls who are reluctant to place their complete trust in Him? O, Disciple who is Attentive to His Teaching, today, lay your request at the throne of grace, knowing, believing, and trusting that you will receive for what you have asked of your loving Father, who is love itself.

PRAYER

Father,
whose hands are full and who longs to pour forth,
I am ready to step into and live from the place of faith,
trusting in you for all I need, believing you will provide.
Jesus,
increase my faith.
Holy Spirit,
teach me to pray.
Teach me to ask big, to trust big, and to believe that I will receive.
I want to be a man or woman of faith in your care, your power, and your provision
In Jesus' name.
Amen

ACTION

- Make a list of those things of which you are going to lay before the Father and trust Him for those needs being met.
- With whom and what will you share from today's lesson?

REFLECTION QUESTIONS

What do you find to be some of the most amazing claims and promises of the Gospel?

Do you believe that your prayers of trust are "safe" or do you place big demands on God?

Why is *"believe to receive"* important to the spiritual life, the life of the sons and daughters of God?

In what areas have you not believed in the Father's loving providence?

FURTHER READING

Romans 8:31

Hebrews 11:6

Luke 12:32

Mark 9:24

Luke 17:5-6

PRAYER HELP: Distractions

"Sean, your dad is praying. Don't bother him," is a loving thing for a wife to say as she sees her two-year-old son crawling all over his dad as he was kneeling to pray. That was a huge moment in my spiritual life. I was around 26 years old and had been seriously pursuing the spiritual life since I was 15 years old. I had read about the dangers of not fighting distractions in prayer and found myself guilty over and over. I had taken the advice of the masters and came to be spending most of my time fighting distractions rather than praying.

I folded to the floor and Sean snuggled up upon my lap. In that moment, I was faced with a decision which would change my spiritual life. As a husband and father, was my son a distraction to my relationship with the Lord? Right as the question crossed my thoughts, grace flooded my soul and infused it with insight. Here is what I saw:

I am a priest and as a priest, I am to take creation with me.
I am a son and as a son, all my life is precious to my Father.

Our father Adam was the first priest of *Elohim*, God the Creator. It was his ministry to gather the gift creation, which he was given by the Father, and return it in a sacrifice of praise. Whenever Adam prayed it was as if all of creation was crying out, *"Take me with you!"* In my baptism, I was anointed as a priest. Whenever I pray, creation stands waiting to see if I will go with empty or full hands. As my son Sean was crawling on me, his spirit was saying, *"Take me with you!"* On that day all distractions ceased, for everything that came to me as I prayed, I took with me to him. Instead of things pulling me from him, they became the things that took me to him. There was nothing I held back from my Father. As his son, I knew that all my life was precious to him and he desired to share in every event, every thought and every concern. Through my anointing as priest and my action of taking all with me, the simplest things became stepping stones to be with him.

Now when I pray, and a thought comes to me, I do not fight the thought as if it was my enemy or as if my Father was disdained by it. What comes to me is what I take to him and thus, I sanctify my life and present it as a sacrifice of praise to the One who gave the gift.

Does this mean I abandon what I was praying and move on to what has entered my mind? No, I just pull it into my prayer. And when I have taken it to the Father, I return to my first prayer.

DAY
NINTEEN

Day 19: Saying to See

"Have faith in God," Jesus answered. "I tell you the truth, if anyone says to this mountain, 'Go, throw yourself into the sea,' and does not doubt in his heart but believes that what he says will happen, it will be done for him. Mark 11:22-23

MEDITATION

One thing that I have noticed is that the Kingdom of God is in many ways opposite to the ways in which we live, or, more accurately stated, the way in which we live is opposite as compared to the Kingdom – give and you shall receive, lose your life and you will find it, and so on. We see something and say what it is. In the Kingdom, it is the opposite of this. In the Kingdom, we say something so it may come to be as Jesus has taught in his *School of Prayer*.

Here is a formidable and alarming revelation to grasp: the power of life and death are in your tongue; the power of creation and destruction are in your tongue, and the power of blessing and cursing are in your tongue. Do not underestimate, Son or Daughter of God, the authority that comes forth from your mouth. Stand with awe and respect that of which you are capable, simply by your words, and begin to choose carefully what you confess with your lips. Whisper your words and without the lifting of your hand, lives can be destroyed. In the same, whisper your words and lives can be blessed and exalted as you stand in the distance and watch those words fulfilled. What wonderment should come to our hearts when we examine that which our words have created and our words have destroyed. Listen to someone who has faced the verbal abuse of another, especially from the lips of a dad, and you will be solidified in the truth of the tongue's power. Conversely, be attentive to someone who was encouraged by the words of others, especially a dad, and you will know, beyond doubt, that the tongue should be given more honor than it is assigned.

Jesus knew this truth. But it was not from human behavior alone. He knew this truth because it is he who set forth this principle in the act of creation. He spoke and there was light. He spoke and there was all that is. He spoke. In this, we see the way of the functioning of the cosmos, a law of creation, which, though we deny it, still has its way. One can deny gravity but step off the cliff and the denier quickly becomes a believer, if there is enough time. The Law of Say and See is just as much a reality as all that Newton dreamed.

In the *School of Prayer,* Jesus instructs his disciples to speak to the mountain and command it to do what it is commanded to do. Notice that this is not the Prayer of Request, a supplication, but rather, the Prayer of Command. By the Prayer of Command, the son or daughter of God speaks in the name of Jesus with Jesus' authority, and what is spoken is seen to be. The Prayer of Command places the power and authority of Jesus in the tongue of the believer. With the Prayer of Command, the believer speaks to cancer, commands it to shrivel and die, and casts the spirit of cancer into the pits of hell, releases life and health into the body, and all are done for the glory of the Father. The Prayer of Command empowers the redeemed to stand in the face of the onslaught of hell and release angelic, warring angels to battle on behalf of the holy ones. The stance of the one speaking to that which is the Father's will to manifest, is not earth to heaven, but heaven released into the earth. There is a time when we are waiting on heaven to act, but many times it is the time when heaven is waiting for us to act with the authority and power which has been given through the name of Jesus. Son or Daughter of Light, I wonder what has been waiting for your command to be loosed on earth?

The Law of Say and See, coupled with the name of Jesus, is the hope of our Father to partner with man to bring about the Kingdom on earth.

PRAYER

Abba, my Father,
you spoke and all came to be.
Thank you for the power of words.
Jesus,
I repent of all times that I have used words to bring a curse rather than a blessing, death rather than life.
I choose life!
Holy Spirit,
teach me to pray.
Set a guard over my mouth that I might speak as you would speak.
In Jesus' name.
Amen

ACTION

- For three days, challenge yourself to not say one thing negative to or about someone, but instead, look for ways to speak words that build up others.

96

- With whom and what will you share from today's lesson?

REFLECTION QUESTIONS

What are the words you have spoken which have created and built up?

What are words you have spoken that have broken and torn down?

What things do you need to speak to with authority and start commanding, in the name of Jesus?

FURTHER READING

Proverbs 18:21

Psalm 63:3

Mark 16:17

2 Timothy 1:7

John 14:12

Day 20: Prayer for Him to Provide

Give us this day our daily bread. Lk 11:3

MEDITATION

I opened the fridge, and it was empty. My first thought, *"This is a good time to clean the fridge"*

As I cleaned I thought, *"I am famished for a steak."* But that was wishful thinking as we did not even have enough to buy bread or sliced, plastic wrapped cheese for grilled cheese sandwiches, let alone steak. We did have some potatoes which were starting to root and, of course, ketchup and mustard. When there is little in the fridge, it is brightly lit and easy to clean.

Dinner came, and we sat at the empty table. We joined hands and prayed, *"Bless us, O Lord, and these thy gifts which we are ABOUT to receive from thy bounty, through Christ, our Lord, Amen!"*

Knock! Knock!

I ran to the door, opened it to find no one there. We lived in an apartment on the second floor which allowed us to oversee the entire apartment complex, but there was no one to be seen. To the right of the door were six, overflowing bags of groceries which we scooped up while yelling out at the top of my voice, *"Thank you, whoever you are!"* We took our "feast to be" to the kitchen. Into the first bag I reached and pulled out – RIBEYE STEAKS. If you are the giver of those grocery bags and you are reading this, I wish you would have stayed and joined us for dinner. Thank you for your love.

In 1996, I had the opportunity to give away everything that I owned and begin to live a life of full-time service to the Kingdom, depending on the goodness of God through his good people. The Father spoke to my heart that if I took care of his house, the Church, he would take care of mine. As I write, that was 21 years ago. We have trusted the Father, my *AhDah*, for everything for 21 years. If you could see me, you would see a man that is nicely insulated for the winter, and you would know from the thickness of the insulation that there is a God who is his loving *Dad*. I know my Father is real and that his promises are true because I have had to rely on him for all our needs for all these years and he has always been faithful to fulfill his word to me.

This I know. Our Father cares about every area of our life. As a Father, he provides, protects, and guides. I am a dad, and I love it when I have the opportunity to provide, protect, and guide my children. Being a dad is not something that I do. Being a dad is who I am. It is the same with God, our loving Father. He is glorified when we allow him to be who he is – a provider, protector, and guide. It is good for you to go to him with all your needs and wants. Do not ever think like a pagan. Over the years I have heard people say, *"He has more important things to attend to than my little needs."* This statement is true if our god is Zeus who is an exalted human being. Our Father is not Zeus. Our Father is All-powerful. There is nothing big or small for him and he can do all at once and nothing is taken from him when he does something for us. Besides, because he is love, all your concerns are of equal value and importance to him, O Son or Daughter.

The Early Church Fathers also understood *"Daily Bread"* to apply to the Eucharist. Our greatest hunger is for God. In the depth of our being, everything in us longs for union with Him. This longing for union we have is because God is longing and yearning for us. God is hungry for us. In the Old Testament, God made covenant with man. Many of us confuse covenant with contract. A covenant is an exchange of persons. It sounds like this , *"I am yours, and you are mine."* A contract is an exchange of goods or services. A contract is limited in relationship and comes to an end once the goods and services are exchanged or when they are not exchanged the contract is broken and terminated. A covenant is for the life of the persons who have entered into it. In the Old Testament, God, *Yahweh*, was a spirit who made a spiritual covenant with man.

In Christ Jesus, God has become man and taken on a body. Knowing that covenant is an exchange of persons, with God becoming incarnate in Jesus, a New Covenant, a new exchange of persons was needed so that Jesus could give his entire self – body, soul, and spirit – to us. Therefore, at the Last Supper, Jesus took bread and wine and changed it into his body and blood, the New Covenant, so that all believers in all ages could receive him completely and entirely. Communion, the Eucharist, is not meant to be just a spiritual reality or we would still be making a covenant with God in the same way that it was done before the coming of Jesus. Communion must be and truly is Jesus' body, blood, soul, and divinity. It is not a symbol. It is really and substantially him based on his words. At the Mass, one is able is receive the "total Christ" and not just part of him.

At the Mass, the greatest longing of every human soul is able to be fulfilled and that longing is union with God.

At the Mass, Jesus Christ, our daily bread, says, *"Here I am, totally and completely. I long for you. Take and eat. Take and drink. Now, I am unreservedly yours."*

In the Mass, the soul says back to Jesus, *"Here I am, totally and completely. I long for you. Take and eat. Take and drink. This is my body. This is my blood. Now, I am unreservedly yours."*

One must ask, who is consuming whom when communion is received?

Disciple of Jesus, present to your Father your daily needs knowing that it glorifies him when you do so, but know that your greatest need, your greatest longing, is for him. May your heart swell with a profound hunger to be consumed by him and to consume him at the next Mass.

PRAYER

Father, *Yahweh Yireh,*
you are my provider, protector, and my guide.
Thank you for wanting to know my needs and desires.
I lay them before you.
Jesus,
thank you for coming to me to meet my greatest need, my greatest longing which is for you.
Thank you for giving yourself to me totally and completely in the Eucharist.
Help me to hunger for you as you hunger for me.
I am yours!
Holy Spirit,
teach me to pray.
Increase my hunger and desire for Jesus, our Eucharistic Lord, the Bread of Life come down from heaven.
In Jesus' name.
Amen

ACTION

- Commit to being at Mass every Sunday from this day forward and, if you have the chance, attend daily Mass.
- With whom and what will you share from today's lesson?

REFLECTION QUESTIONS

What needs or wants have you withheld from placing before your loving Father?

What do you think or how does it make you feel to know that God is your provider, protector, and guide?

If you were to explain the Eucharist to someone, how would you?

Have you had any experience of encountering Jesus in receiving communion?

FURTHER READING

James 4:2-3

Genesis 17:1-8

John 6:47-59

Luke 22:20

DAY
TwenTy-One

Day 21: Honesty and Acceptance

"Abba, Father," he said, "everything is possible for you. Take this cup from me. Yet not what I will, but what you will." Mark 14:36

MEDITATION

There are times when life just is not as we want it to be. Life can be hurtful, painful, disappointing, discouraging... I am sure you could add to this list. I am sorry for all the times life has been so, for you. We are on this side of Eden, and the Kingdom of God is not fully in our midst. In heaven, all our hopes and longings will be fulfilled, but here, on the earth, they will only partially come to be. To believe otherwise is to add a greater pain amidst pain.

Jesus, in his *School of Prayer,* has shown us in his time of prayer, in the Garden of Gethsemane, how we are to pray when we are facing what we wish could be different.

The first step Jesus shows us is that of a son who is honest with his Father about what he wants. Jesus does not pretend that all is well with him, even as to how he views the Father's will. Jesus is not polyannic. He sees things as they are. Jesus is realistic in his prayer to his Father. He sees that what is about to happen to him will be extremely painful and he does not want to face the pain. Jesus wanted his Father to take the cup of suffering from him.

Jesus enters into the second phase of his prayer. It is only after Jesus has been honest with his *Abba* about the suffering which he is about to face that he can enter into the next stage of his prayer which is that of surrender. Our Father loves us so much that he respects what we are experiencing. Our *Abba* is not an overlord who cares only that we do his will. He sees us and what we are facing as we grow into his will and he comes with his grace to help us make the step of acceptance. Here is the truth we find as we gaze into this moment of Jesus' life. It is the truth that we cannot, of ourselves, do God's will. We need God's grace to do God's will, and he is ever ready to give that grace. It takes the faith of a child to walk with our Father, and child-like faith requires of us that we need him for all that he asks of us.

There is a difference between acceptance and resignation in the spiritual life. Acceptance is the union of wills. As the will of one grows into the will of the Other, the grace of surrender is given. Contrary to acceptance is resignation. Resignation is allowing the will of the other to dominate one's conflicting will. Resignation is not the union of wills. Resignation is submission to the will of the other. Our Father does not want for souls to submit to him. Our Father wishes for sons and daughter who will accept the gift of his will. He is love, and as love, he desires that we surrender to his will. Surrender flows from trust. The more one progresses in intimacy, the more one will trust, and with that trust, the more one can surrender to the Other. The heart that yields to the Father's will knows that at all times the Father wants only the greater good for that soul.

Son or Daughter of the Father, given the nature and character of our Father, our *Abba*, it truly makes senses to surrender to his will and desire his will as your own.

Our *Papa* is all knowing and can see what lies ahead for us and what will help us become all that we were created to be. We are finite in our knowledge and imagination so we cannot see where our road is taking us. Son or Daughter of the Father, surrender to your Father who knows all.

Son or Daughter of the Father, your *Abba* is wise. He knows how to bring about the perfection of your soul. We have glimpses of what is best for us, but even those glimpses are a gift of his grace which allows us to see the ultimate good. Son or Daughter of the Father, surrender to the will of your wise Father.

Son or Daughter of the Father, your Father is good. In him there is no darkness. Because he is good, he only wants your good. We can be confused as to what is good for us because of our immaturity. We seek the easy path which brings quick results, but it is not the path that offers all we need to become all that we could become. Your Father designs all in your life to work for your good, if you but trust him. Son or daughter of the Father, surrender to the will of your all good Father.

PRAYER

Father, my *Abba*,
I trust you.
I surrender all that I am and all that I have to your will,
knowing that you are willing what is best for me.
Thank you for your will.
Jesus,
bring my will into union with the Father's will.
Holy Spirit,

teach me to pray.
I give you my will.
In Jesus' name.
Amen

ACTION

- Make a list of what you want out of life for yourself and those you love. Take that list before the tabernacle and leave it there as a sign of surrender of your will to the Father's will.
- With whom and what will you share from today's lesson?

REFLECTION QUESTIONS

What are difficulties you are facing in life?

Are there situations in your life of which you are fearful?

What are your thoughts or feelings about doing the Father's will?

Are there any areas of your life where you are resisting the Father's will?

FURTHER READING

John 16:33

2 Corinthians 12:8-10

1 Samuel 3:18

Romans 12:1-3

Romans 8:28

PRAYER HELPS: Personality and Spirituality

Two things stand true for the foundation of the spiritual life:

1. *Know thyself.* We are called to give ourselves to the Lord for we are what he desires.
2. *Grace builds on nature.* This means that God takes what is and enhances it to the level of divine life with the infusion of grace.

There are many methods to type personalities. The Myers-Briggs Temperament Indicator (MBTI) is a scientific method to determine the composition of one's personality. The MBTI proposes 16 different temperaments with four base personalities.

The most common personality (believed to be 50% of the population of those who go to church) is that of the combinations of the Sensing/Judging personality. This is also the most common spirituality type promoted by Christian spiritual teachers, given it is the highest percentage of Church-going population. This personality is also the type that is best at organizing people and methods. The spirituality type that is associated with the SJ temperament is that of the Jesuits (the SJ of Myers-Briggs is a coincidence in comparison with the SJ, Society of Jesus, of the Jesuits). Saint Ignatius', the founder of the Jesuits, main way of seeing the spiritual life was through the lens of an army about to go into a spiritual battle.

Given that SJ personality/spirituality is 50% of the population of believers, it also stands that the other 50% of the Christian community does not find this as their primary way of approaching God. Half of believers have been taught a way of prayer that is foreign to their personality. When they practice the way of the SJ personality, it does not fit. They feel as though they are failures. This does not disparage the SJ personality. It just means that SJ have more support for their natural way of prayer while others need to search.

Given our two dictums with which we started, as we know our personality and practice the path from which our spirituality naturally springs, then grace will come and make us more like Christ.

For a deeper understanding read ***Prayer and Temperament: Different Prayer Forms for Different Personality Types*** by Chester P. Michael and Marie C. Norrisey

Temperament/Spirituality Step in Lectio Divina	Methods
SJ (Ignatian)	Regimented, Structured, Observation, Ritual, Will
Lectio – to read	Lectio – as the passage is read one places oneself in the scene.
NT (Thomistic)	Desire to Understand, Neat, Orderly, Seeks: Goodness, Unity, Truth, Beauty, Study, Intellect
Lectio – to meditate	Lectio – ponders the meaning of what was read and seeks understanding.
SP (Franciscan)	Free-flowing, Creation-based, Service, Spontaneous Praise, Celebration, Eclectic, Will, Intellect, Emotion (Whatever works)
Lectio – to pray	Lectio – Feels and talks to God about what was read
NF (Augustinian)	Imaginative, Creative, Mystical, Finds Meaning, Experiences God's Love in the Present, Quiet Emotion
Lectio – to contemplate	Lectio – what is read causes one to hear in one's soul and experience union.

DAY
Twenty-Two

Day 22: Boldness in Prayer

Then he said to them, "Suppose one of you has a friend, and he goes to him at midnight and says, 'Friend, lend me three loaves of bread, because a friend of mine on a journey has come to me, and I have nothing to set before him.'

"Then the one inside answers, 'Don't bother me. The door is already locked, and my children are with me in bed. I can't get up and give you anything.' I tell you, though he will not get up and give him the bread because he is his friend, yet because of the man's boldness he will get up and give him as much as he needs. Luke 11:5-8

MEDITATION

Years ago, when I was in my early twenties and wanted to get rich, I knew I needed to start somewhere. So I thought that being a salesman with a strong, proven corporation would be a good stepping stone. I searched the paper to see what I could find. There it was, the perfect job. It had a good base and an excellent opportunity for commission since it was a nationally known company that was at the top of its field. There could have been a problem if I would have considered the fact that I did not meet the experience and education requirements. I called the local cooperate office and found out the name of the president of sales. I called back and asked for him. He answered the phone and I told him that I wanted to interview with him for the open position. Of course, he told me to call their HR person.

I went on to sell myself. He bought my pitch of self and offered me a personal interview. On the way to the appointment, I started to think about my inexperience and that I was meeting with someone of such power. I started to sweat. I turned to my AhDah, my Father, about my reticence. He immediately spoke to my heart, "Why are you afraid of that man? You come into my presence, the Creator of all, the One who is All-powerful. And you come to me without fear. So why are you afraid of this man? Go in there and get that job!"

I walked into the president's office as if I were walking into the throne room of heaven. I greeted him with a firm handshake. After a brief discussion, he offered me the job. There I was in a cheap suit, with no experience and the wrong education. Yet, I had an amazing job on which to build my future. I asked him why he chose to hire me and he said, *"You are bold and did anything you could to get this job. I know you will be bold and do anything you can to make us money."*

I was bold because I knew who I was and I knew who my Father is. This is how we are to approach prayer. We are his sons and daughters, Jesus has given us all we need, so we need to approach the throne of grace to ask and receive all we need to bring his Kingdom into the earth.

In baptism, each of us was anointed priest, prophet, and king. The anointing is done with sacred chrism oil and is a sign of the empowerment anointing of the Holy Spirit for the believer to accomplish the task to which the believer is called. This anointing speaks to us of our ministries in the Kingdom of God.

Priest – Raises his hands to heaven to bless *Yahweh* and then lowers his hands to the earth to bless the people. A priest stands between God and others to offer worship in their place and to make intercession for their needs.

Prophet – Turns his ear to God to hear his word and then speaks that word to the people.

King – Brings God's rule and reign into the earth, overcoming the works of the kingdom of darkness to establish the Kingdom of God.

In this parable, Jesus tells of a man who comes to his friend, literally to a *brother*, and asks for supply so that he can help another friend, a *brother*. The one who makes the request for help knows two things about the one he is approaching: 1) He is a *brother,* and as a *brother,* he knows of his friend's heart, which is filled with kindness and generosity. He is not timid to ask his friend because he knows the one to whom he is making his plea. Because of their *brotherhood,* he is bold in his asking, no matter the need and no matter the hour. 2) The one making the request also knows that his *brother* has what he needs. He is not approaching someone who is scarce in his supply. He stands before a friend, a *brother,* who has been blessed and he, being bound to him in *brotherhood,* knows that because of their bond, his *brother's* supply is also his supply and, therefore, he can be bold in his request.

This last statement, "his *brother's* supply is also his supply", is a radical approach to God and to our relationship with each other as believers who have become sons and daughters of God, brothers and sisters through the waters of baptism, with the same Father who is *Abba*.

109

In the *School of Prayer,* we are constantly brought back to realizing the identity of God, our good, generous, loving Father and our identity in Christ Jesus. Because of Jesus, we are friends of God. His abundant grace has made us *brothers* with Jesus. What Jesus has is ours. He holds nothing back from us. He even gives us his body and blood in the Eucharist so that we can totally and completely possess him. Knowing that what belongs to Jesus, our *brother,* is ours, we should be bold and not afraid or timid to make demand upon all that he has.

When we pray as a priest, we pray for ourselves and for others. Here, we see a *brother* praying for the needs of his *brother.* As believers, we are called to make intercession for the world. We are surrounded by those who need *bread,* that which will truly feed them. And we have the responsibility to go to the One who has the *bread* they need and boldly ask for that *bread.* We should not be cocky or sheepish in our approach to God. We come before him as a son or daughter on the behalf of those he loves and those whom we are called to love. It is love that brings us into his presence to press in for the need of our friend. Love is daring.

O Disciple, see those around you who are hungry and do not withhold from them that which you can obtain. Go you to your *Abba* who is *El Shaddai* and place on him an unrelenting demand for all they need and watch him act as a friend and *brother.*

PRAYER

Father, the provider for all,
thank you that you always hear my prayer and you always give me
access into your presence.
I come for those who are hungry knowing you can meet their needs and I
am grateful that you are ready to be the friend of my friend.
Jesus,
You have brought me into your relationship with the Father.
Thank you!
Holy Spirit,
teach me how to pray.
It is you who have anointed me as a royal priest.
Teach me how to enter that priesthood and make intercession for those
in need with great boldness and confidence.
In Jesus' name.
Amen

ACTION

- The next time you stand in prayer, lift your hands to heaven and spend time blessing the Lord and then lower your hands to the earth to start interceding for others.
- With whom and what will you share from today's lesson?

REFLECTION QUESTIONS

Which aspect of the anointing of your baptism do you see yourself exercising the most - priest, prophet or king?

What do you think or how does it make you feel to know that you can approach God as a friend?

What do you think or how does it make you feel to know that you can approach God with boldness?

What are some needs of others for which you need to boldly approach God about?

FURTHER READING

1 Peter 2:9

Ephesians 1:3

Genesis 18:16-33

Hebrews 7:25

DAY
Twenty-Three

Day 23: Answered Prayer Brings Glory to the Father

"...because I am going to the Father. And I will do whatever you ask in my name, so that the Son may bring glory to the Father. You may ask me for anything in my name, and I will do it." John 14:12-13

MEDITATION

Imagine eight kids opening presents on Christmas morning and friends invited over to share the joy. That is our house. I was an only child, so the opening of presents went lickety-split. My wife Andrea's has one older brother, Jimmy, and one younger sister, Pam. They went around the room and one person at a time opened gift as all watched. We have established the tradition of doing the same and I love it. With eight kids it takes us at least two hours, if not more. I must say, as a dad, it is so fun to sit back and watch. One at a time, the kids will open a present and everyone will rejoice with them in what they received. All year long, Andrea is listening to hear what they like and she is amazing about making sure they get what they forgot to put on their letter to Santa. As parents, when all is said and done, we sit back and enjoy our children's joy and this brings us glory.

Jesus loves answering our prayer, yes, because he loves us, but, more importantly, he answers our prayers for in doing so, it brings glory to his Father, just as watching my kids enjoy the blessings I give them brings me glory. Jesus is always desiring to bring his Father the glory he rightly deserves.

When we pray we should pray with great confidence that our prayers will be answered, knowing that Jesus longs to bring glory to the Father. Of course, we are not going to ask for something which offends the way of holiness. Jesus says that if we ask for anything he will do it to bring the Father glory. Let us hear clearly, Jesus says *"anything"*. I swear, most of us insert a footnote to this saying of Jesus about prayer, writing in our minds, *"But do not ask for this and do not ask for this. This is not covered by 'anything', so do not ask."* Son or daughter of your *Daddy,* who is God, Jesus is waiting, right now, to hear your prayer and is waiting to bring it to pass. In every moment, his heart is consumed with what he can do to worship the Father. Lift up your prayers and let him come to your aid so he might display the Father's magnificence. His ear is attentive to your cry so that in fulfilling it he might shout the Father's praise.

Even when the unbeliever is blessed, he is blessed through the hands of Jesus. And even if that one does not give thanks to the Father for the blessing he has received, Jesus stands before the throne as the faithful son who is about his Father's business, worshiping his Father for the blessing that was not acknowledged. Jesus leads the worship of heaven. Day and night, all of heaven is crying out, led by Jesus, in adoration of his most generous Father. Imagine how many blessings are upon your life every day. There are more blessings you receive of which you will never know in this life than the ones which you do know. Jesus, the worship leader of heaven, the one who has interceded for you to have those blessings, worships the Father for each one you have received. Day and night, Jesus cries out,

All glory and honor are yours, Almighty Father, forever and ever.

This is what is happening in every celebration of the Mass. When we celebrate Mass, we are not getting heaven to join our worship, we are joining in the heavenly worship with myriad upon myriad who shout his praise. Once the Holy Spirit said to me, as we were celebrating the Holy Sacrifice of Praise, the Mass,

"If your physical ears were opened, right now, to hear the heavenly worship which surrounds you, you would go deaf."

A popular misconception of heaven is that of a pastoral scene with beautiful flowers, trees, a running stream, and a little cherub, softly playing a harp. Being quiet or speaking with hushed tones is our definition of reverence. This is not the heaven which has been revealed by the Holy Spirit. The revealed heaven is one of joyful acclamation where the host are shouting like peals of thunder, like a mighty ocean roar. One of the Hebrew words for praise, *teruwah*, means to *"split the ear."* If you ever worship next to my brother, Nick Villalobos, you will understand the Hebrew meaning of this word. He is so joyously loud that it pierces your ear. I love to stand next to Nick and join him in turning up the volume of the praise. Yikes, then bring in Gabe and Pam Castellanos, Efrain Roman, Benjamin Ziemann, Nick Baron, and Saul and Maite Perez. When you get all these brothers and sisters together, ear plugs will be required.

O Disciple, the joy that should fill our hearts when our prayer is answered and the thanksgiving we should render unto our most generous *Abba*. How could we not sing? How could we not dance? How could we not wave our hands, clap, and shout his praise? Some would say this is irreverent. Then I ask, are they irreverent in heaven? For these are the same displays of his praise which they use.

PRAYER

Father,
from whose hand, every good and perfect gift comes from above,
thank you.
Thank you for all the blessings which I know and the countless more of which I do not know.
Jesus,
help me to be humble and lay my every request before you that you might answer my prayer and bring glory to your Father.
Holy Spirit,
teach me to pray.
Help me to stand before you with the great expectancy of answered prayer.
In Jesus' name.
Amen

ACTION

- Write a list of answered prayers and enter into a time of worship of the Father for each one of your answered prayers. Push yourself into a place of praise to which you have never gone.
- With whom and what will you share from today's lesson?

REFLECTION QUESTIONS

What is something you do for others that brings you glory when they enjoy your gift?

What is your gut reaction to Jesus saying that he will do anything we ask in his name so as to bring glory to his Father?

How do you feel about joyful, exuberant worship? Where could you go to enjoy and grow in it?

Has this lesson changed your image of heaven?

FURTHER READING

Psalm 9:1

Psalm 107:8-9

Revelation 4:6-11

Colossians 3:17

Revelation 19:1-10

DAY
Twenty-Four

Day 24: Your Life, His Will

Then I said, "Here I am - it is written about me in the scroll - I have come to do your will, my God." Hebrews 10:7

MEDITATION

I am so blessed to be married to my wife, Andrea. I always tell people, as I preach around the US, to pray for our marriage. My voice gets somber and my pace slows down as I tell them, *"We do not have a good marriage."* I stare at them and they return the gaze with sympathy to which I respond, *"Yeah, we do not have a good marriage. We have an excellent marriage and I need you to pray that we keep it that way."* You can hear the room sigh and some are jeering at me. They take it hook, line and sinker every time and I giggle. We do have a fantastic marriage. I know that it is a gift and I am grateful to the gift giver, our Father.

Love is the union of wills and it is seeking the will of the other. One of the things which makes our marriage so strong is that both of us are always in search of and enjoying the doing of the will of the other. Andrea lives a very sacrificial life for me to fulfill the call of God on my life. She not only does this out of love for the Father, but she knows that I am alive when I am ministering the gospel all over the country. And now, the world is opening to me. She lays down her will and encourages me to go and preach the Gospel to all the nations because she knows that I was created for the proclamation and demonstration of the Kingdom. I love you, Andrea, and I am so grateful for all you sacrifice for the Kingdom and for me. Thank you, Baby!

The union of wills and the seeking of the will of the Father, doing his will with enjoyment, must be the essence of our love for the Father. We see this reflected in the life of Jesus. Today's Scripture illuminates for us what Jesus said as he was coming into the world. As he left the Father's throne, his prayer to his *Abba* is recorded in this passage.

There are two parts to the prayer of Jesus as he descends into the womb of the Virgin Mary to become the Incarnate Word, the God-Man. These two parts are a lesson for us in the *School of Prayer.*

The first lesson is that of total oblation, meaning, the giving of self to the other. Jesus presents himself to his Father as a gift – *"Here I am."* In the *School of Prayer,* our first stance when we come to prayer is to offer our lives as a living sacrifice. It is the sound of surrender; it is the sound of lovers, and it speaks the words,

"All I am and all I have is yours."

Disciple of Jesus, learn from listening to the prayer of your humble Master, the first steps in prayer. It is the way of giving, of self-sacrifice, oblation, abandonment to the other. And in this way we see the way of love. Let our hearts start our time of prayer, exclaiming with deep longing,

"I am yours! I am yours! Take my life! I am yours!"

Now that we have given ourselves, we can then move to the next stage, which is desiring the will of the Other. Surrender leads to doing that for which we were created to do, which is the giving of self. Jesus, on departing the presence of his Father proclaims as he takes on flesh,

"I have come to do your will."

During my college years I taught guitar. The best student I had was Joey, a young man who was mentally handicapped. Joey, without being asked, would make a chart of his practice sessions. When we began our lesson, Joey would give me his chart displaying an hour of practice every day. I had to grade his chart, and without fail, Joey would get an A+ with a star. For our lessons, I would draw out what is called a chord chart. Joey would place his fingers upon the frets and then strum. Once, we followed these steps, and when Joey drew his pick across the strings, there was dissidence, meaning it did not sound too good and Joey could tell. I told him to reexamine the chart and try again. The result was the same. After three attempts, I took hold of his fingers to move them to the right places on the fret board. But Joey's fingers were stiff and resistant to my moving. I looked at him and asked, *"Joe, do you know how to play the guitar?"* With a look of gazing at a fool he answered, *"No, that is why I am paying you to teach me."* With firmness I spoke, *"Then relax your fingers and let me put them where they should go."* Joey let go of the control of his hand and allowed me to place his fingers on the frets, he strummed and joy came to his face, for he knew it sounded good. This is the way of the spiritual life: we relax into the hands of God so that he might use our life to do his will and to bring harmony to a discordant world.

O disciple of Jesus, let this be your pray upon your rising,

Father, I am yours. Take my life and do with it as you will.

PRAYER

Father, my Father,
I am yours and yours I wish to be.
Take my life and do with it as you will.
I withhold nothing from you.
All I am and all I have is yours.
Jesus,
You lived a life of total abandonment to your Father's will.
Teach me to do the same.
Holy Spirit,
teach me to pray.
I am too small and too weak.
Be my strength to do that which I cannot do.
In Jesus' name.
Amen

ACTION

- For one week, start your day by falling with your face to the floor, your arms spread like a cross, and in your own words, give everything you are and everything you have to your Father. Then rise to your knees, with the same outstretched arms and proclaim your life is for his will.
- With whom and what will you share from today's lesson?

REFLECTION QUESTIONS

Have you ever given your life as a sacrifice, an offering to God?

What do you think would be the benefit of living your life in uniformity with the will of God?

Who do you know that lives a life of surrender to the Lord Jesus and God the Father? What is it about their life that tells you they live a surrendered life?

FURTHER READING

1 Corinthians 10:24

Philippians 2:4

Romans 12:1-3

Proverbs 23:26

Psalm 40:8

Day 25: Persistence in Prayer

Then Jesus told his disciples a parable to show them that they should always pray and not give up. He said: "In a certain town there was a judge who neither feared God nor cared about men. And there was a widow in that town who kept coming to him with the plea, 'Grant me justice against my adversary.'

"For some time, he refused. But finally he said to himself, 'Even though I don't fear God or care about men, yet because this widow keeps bothering me, I will see that she gets justice, so that she won't eventually wear me out with her coming!'" And the Lord said, "Listen to what the unjust judge says. And will not God bring about justice for his chosen ones, who cry out to him day and night? Will he keep putting them off? I tell you, he will see that they get justice, and quickly. However, when the Son of Man comes, will he find faith on the earth?" Luke 18:1-8

MEDITATION

Writing about the Lord and his ways is something that comes quite easily to me. I sit down, put my fingers to the keyboard, and the thoughts, without effort, flow out from me on to the screen *(You might be reading this and agree that my writing is effortless and that is your clue as to why it should be better. Grant me some mercy!).*

Effortless? Except for this lesson. I have struggled and struggled to come up with a story or illustration. I changed my venue for writing hoping that would inspire me. To the coffee shop I went. I set up my laptop, ready to be inspired. But all I came home with was caffeine jitters. Every time I have prayed for the Holy Spirit to guide me and there was nothing, flat, blah. I have tried to figure out how to scrap this lesson on persistence in prayer by searching for a saying of Jesus to replace this one, but I knew I had to keep pushing onward given that Jesus said that persistence is how we should pray. I could not give up. With each sitting, I prayed and re-read the saying of Jesus. My soul kept saying, *"Brendan, do not give up. Persist. Continue the course. Persevere."*

I am sure that by now you see what I was not seeing. My experience in writing this lesson is the experience of what the Lord Jesus is saying. Duh! Well, good luck in what you are about to read. Hopefully, my persistaence and not giving up will bear fruit.

In the *School of Prayer,* the same Jesus that tells us that if we pray, believing, that we will receive, realizes that there are times when we have to press in and keep coming to God with our plea. One of the lessons we need to learn in the *School* is to pray and not give up *(or, in my case, write and not give up).*

There are two types of postures when we pray:

The Prayer of Childlike Faith
The Prayer of Pressing In

The *Prayer of Childlike Faith* is a faith of standing before the Father receiving all in trust from his loving hands. In the Kingdom, there is a time for this stance of faith. It is a time of complete rest, open surrender. *Childlike Faith* knows the goodness of the Father and relies on that goodness. *Childlike Faith* has no care or fret for it knows that the Father sees all and will do all for his children. This type of faith is effortless and requires only the action of God, once he has our surrender.

The *Prayer of Pressing In* is just as valid in the Kingdom of God and requires just as much faith. The *Prayer of Childlike Faith* is the prayer of receiving. The *Prayer of Pressing In* is the prayer of partnering with the Father to bring his will on earth as it is in heaven. This type of prayer involves me struggling not only for the answer for which I pray, but the struggling of me not letting go of the continued prayer. The *Prayer of Pressing In* will cause you to sweat and become tired. This prayer demands something of you and will cost. *The Prayer of Pressing In* is the way of the woman in labor. It does not avoid contractions and back labor; the baby seems as if it has chosen the womb as its permanent home. As the prayer drags on there is even temptation to despair as one waits and waits and waits. Sometimes in this prayer the soul will begin to reason, *"Maybe I should do this or that and if I do this or that then God will respond."* As we hold on, we might endure the enemy whispering in our ear, *"It will never happen. Just give up."* or *"God are you even listening? Do you care?"* Then there is the battle with our flesh which cries out, *"I want what I want and I want it now. My Kingdom come, my will be done on earth as it is in heaven."* All the while the nails of our crucifixion cry to be pulled out so that we will not die to self.

Something more is being offered through *The Prayer of Pressing In* than an answer to our prayer. The *more* is that we are being formed in character. *The Prayer of Pressing In* is making one a Son or Daughter of Faith. When one must be patient, when one has to tarry in hope, then one is more like Jesus in trust of the Father. Faith is easy when the answer is immediate. But when the answer seems as if it will never come, faith becomes faith. *The Prayer of Pressing In* is about the making, the shaping, of you and it determines who you really are.

O disciple of Jesus, do not flinch from being wielded by this powerful tool. Fall into the Potter's Hand and let him mold you into the Son.

PRAYER

Father, merciful Father,
help me to not let go of your promises.
Help me to stand and believe for that which I am persisting.
Jesus,
I believe what you have said.
Help my unbelief.
Holy Spirit,
I am weak.
I need your grace of fortitude.
Strengthen me to not give up.
In Jesus' name.
Amen

ACTION

- Buy Bill Johnson's book, **Strengthen Yourself in the Lord**, and, someday, read it so that you might learn how to face times of waiting and persevering.
- With whom and what will you share from today's lesson?

REFLECTION QUESTIONS

What is the thing for which you have struggled the most in prayer?

How do you feel when your prayer is not answered when you would like it answered?

How could you strengthen yourself in the Lord to make it through times of waiting on the Lord?

Is there anything for which you have given up in prayer to which you need to return?

FURTHER READING

Matthew 18:3

Matthew 11:12

Romans 8:29

Galatians 2:20

DAY

TWENTY-SIX

Day 26: Prayer Partnered with Fasting

And he said to them: This kind can go out by nothing, but by prayer and fasting. Mark 19:29

MEDITATION

I was not feeling well, so I went to the doctor. The cuff was wrapped around my arm and he began to squeeze the bulb. *"Oooo!"* He exclaimed which does not sound so good when your doctor makes that sound. Cautiously I asked, *"What's the problem?"* Shaking his head, he answered, *"Your blood pressure is so high that I really should send you to the emergency room."* I told him that I needed to pray. Without thought, I told him that the Holy Spirit told me to go on a 40 day fast where I would just drink water. He said that the fast would fix my high blood pressure and it did. My blood pressure is now, consistently, 120/80. Before the fast it was 210/118.

How was I going to make it for 40 days on just water? I had a problem exercising my will to fast for 24 hours let alone for 40 days. I learned a secret about life when I was in my mid-twenties. *Don't focus on what you are letting go. Focus on what you are taking hold.*

This principle has carried me through many things which I have not wanted to do in life. It is the same as a woman going through the pain of labor. She endures it so that she might hold her child. My fast would not be about eating; it would be about obtaining the grace to heal cancer. I hate cancer and I would really like the grace to heal it, in Jesus name, in every person living with cancer that I meet. I sent out an email asking people to send me pictures of those they know who are facing cancer or who have died from cancer. I put those pictures on my phone. On day 24 of the fast, the urge to eat was overwhelming me. I was cooking a roast with mashed potatoes and all the fixings for my family. I was whipping the potatoes. They were so creamy. My mouth began to water. No one could see me. All I wanted to do was to taste their delight. No one would know. I could even eat a healthy portion and no one would know. I reached for my phone which I had with me at all times and pulled up a picture of a six-year-old girl who was facing cancer. I had a choice – the grace to heal that beautiful little girl or eat the potatoes. The battle ended. I wanted her to live. It was easy not to eat. I chose her.

125

Day 40 came, and I can tell you that those days of fasting were some of the most powerful days of my life, not because of what I accomplished, but because of what grace accomplished in me.

On Day 13 of this book we learned of how we are spirit, soul, and body. We discovered how the carnal man is dominated by his body *(systems and senses)* and/or his soul *(intellect, will, and emotions)*. This domination of the carnal pulls the spirit *(communion and revelation)* to the things below. We, also, saw how with the spiritual man the soul and body are drawn up into the things above. Prayer and fasting help captivate the body and soul, drawing them into the spirit to drink of the grace (read, *life*) of God. The spiritual man, now in right order, is in communion with God to receive revelation and move with the authority and power of Jesus. Prayer, accompanied by fasting, is one tool to empower the restored man to his destined position in the earth to spread the Kingdom of God.

In the early Church, it was the practice to fast on Wednesdays and Fridays. Throughout the centuries, Friday has become a day of fasting for believers for it is the day when the Lord Jesus suffered and died. For the believing, Friday is a day of penance, the denial of self, for the believer, joining Jesus who died out of love for us. Fasting and other acts of self-denial are practices which grace uses to put and keep us in proper order.

Fasting also trains us to say "no" to our desires so that when the day comes when the denial of our will is required we will have practiced and made ourselves ready to say "yes." This principle is what makes Christian fasting different than the religions of man. Their ascetics fast to empty self and to stay empty. The Christian denies and empties himself that he might be filled. In other words, the Christian says "no" that he might say "yes". Denial in itself is useless in the Kingdom of God. On the other hand, denial to dedicate one's self to the will of God is everything in the Kingdom of God.

There are many types of fasts:
• Water only fast.
• Bread and water fast.
• Vegetable or fruit fast.
• The partial fast which is a fast from sun up to sun down.
• The complete fast which is a fast without food or water.
• Sexual abstinence fast.
• 24 hour fast.
• 10 day fast.
• 3 week fast.
• 40 day fast.
• The corporate fast which is a fast with other believers.

126

PRAYER

Father,
thank you for your grace to offer my body as a weapon of righteousness.
It is my will and desire to be rightly ordered.
I want my spirit to be living in and drawing life from the Holy Spirit.
Jesus,
thank you for the gift you offer me in fasting to partner with you to break
the yoke of oppression, to set the captive free, and release the Kingdom
of God in the earth.
Holy Spirit,
teach me to pray.
Grant me the grace to practice fasting.
In Jesus' name.
Amen

ACTION

- Pray and ask the Holy Spirit when he is calling you to fast, for
  what he is calling you to fast, and how he is calling you to fast?
- With whom and what will you share from today's lesson?

REFLECTION QUESTIONS

Have you ever had the opportunity to fast? What was it like and how did
you see God move?

Why do you think fasting is so important in the Kingdom of God?

Through these lessons, how have you grown in your understanding of the
relationship of spirit, soul, and body?

How would your spiritual life grow if fasting was a regular practice?

FURTHER READING

Hebrews 12:2

Luke 4:2

Matthew 6:17

Joel 1:14

Acts 13:2

Day 27: Spiritual Warfare

At once the Spirit sent him out into the wilderness, and he was in the wilderness forty days, being tempted. Mark 1:12-13

MEDITATION

In the middle of my preaching, a young woman stood up and began to scream. Then her body fell to the floor and began to thrash back and forth. A gasp came from the assembly of believers. I was not going to allow the enemy to get any attention so I asked this woman's husband if he would not mind if we removed her to the cry room in the back of the church where a trained deliverance team could discern and, if it was a demonic infestation, remove the demons and set her free. The husband's eyes filled with tears as he pleaded for help. We came to find out this had happened many times at their home. The woman could not have weighed more than 115 pounds, yet two men could not pick her up. In the end, it took five, large muscle-bound brothers to carry her out of the church.

The People of God stared at me wide-eyed and I could tell that this was a golden opportunity to teach. Here is what I taught:

1. There is no comparison between the power of the enemy and the power of God. One could not say that God is the total size of all creation and the enemy is the size of an atom. This analogy would be in error. There is no comparison which can be made. God, our Father, your *Abba*, is the Creator. He is Infinite, All-powerful, All-knowing, Omnipresent. The enemy and his minions are finite, limited to the power which the Father allows. He is limited to what he can know and what he can reason, and he can only be in one place at one time.

2. Jesus, who is in us, is greater than the enemy, who is in the world. We are not to fear the enemy. We respect his knowledge and power, but we have the knowledge and power of God. It is foolish to taunt or make fun of the enemy. We have been given the authority and power of Jesus to trample on the enemy and send him to the pit.

With that, I returned to my message as the deliverance team went to work cleaning house for the lady in distress. When it came time for the people to come forward for individual prayer ministry, one of the members of the deliverance team approached me, requesting help. Since there was a trained healing team, I went to the cry room at the sister's request, leaving the healing team to minister. No, this was not a three-ring circus. It only had two rings.

When I entered the cry room, it was frigid and I could see my breath. The leader of the team informed me that they were not making progress and asked if I had any ideas. I am trained in deliverance ministry, but it was not my call. I didn't have the possibility of obtaining permission from the pastor. So, I reverted to what I do know – praising God and releasing blessing. As I started to worship, the spirits became agitated. My next step was to start blessing areas of the woman's life. For example:

"Father, you are the Lord of her family. Please bless her parents and her relationship with her parents."

The woman began to swear with great vehemence. When this would happen, I knew that I had hit a stronghold and I would continue to keep blessing that area of her life. Pretty soon, a gush of air would come flying out of her and hit all in the room, and sometimes, it would almost knock us to the ground. There were seven such gusts and we knew that with each, she was being set free. Not only were the leeches melted by the praise of God and the adding of his blessing, but the blessing was filling all the formerly occupied territory with God's presence and grace.

In today's *School of Prayer,* the Lord Jesus himself enters into spiritual warfare with the enemy. Our father Adam was given this earth to bring all creation under the rule of the Kingdom of God. Instead, he yielded creation to the devil and his minions. Lord Jesus, the God-Man, came as the perfect man, the New Adam, to go into battle *(temptation is a battle)* to take back from the enemy that which was lost and restore it to the Father. In the temptation, the evil one thought he could ensnare Jesus into his servitude. Jesus emerges from the desert victorious, initiating the Kingdom of God. Later, he gives the Church the task of spreading his Kingdom to the ends of the earth.

Unavoidable to the Christian life is confronting the enemy or being confronted by him. Every baptized believer has been anointed and empowered by the Holy Spirit to win the battle, be it a personal affront or the taking of territory once ruled by darkness. We do not cower to him; he is to cower to us because of our position in Jesus Christ and our authority to spread the Kingdom.

Our weapons are these – praise, the name of Jesus, the Word of God, and the blood of Jesus. We have been given the helmet of salvation, the breastplate of righteousness, truth as our belt, eagerness to spread the Good News as our foot gear, faith as our shield, and the Word of God as our sword. In our hands are the sacramentals of the Church: the sign of the cross, holy water, blessed salt, the rosary, the medal of Saint Benedict. We have the company of the angels and the Saints who wait for us to call to them for help. In one exorcism after another, these have proven to be hated by the demons.

O Disciple of Jesus, yours is to advance the Kingdom, binding and casting its enemies into the pit. You need not fear for the Lord of Armies, *Yahweh Sabaoth,* is with you. Son and Daughter of the Father, know what you have been given and use all that lies within your grasp.

PRAYER

Father,
yours is the Kingdom and the glory.
Lord Jesus,
thank you for making me your co-heir through the waters of baptism and anointing me with power and strength. I will spread the Kingdom of your Father by overcoming the ways of darkness.
Holy Spirit,
teach me to pray.
When I stand in battle, come and be my helper. Instruct and empower me to bind and cast down the enemy and release your blessings into the earth.
In Jesus' name.
Amen

ACTION

- Think of a sin with which the enemy tempts you and plan your battle response. Assess and revise your plan after every attack, knowing that grace is there for you to win the battle as an overcomer.
- With whom and what will you share from today's lesson?

REFLECTION QUESTIONS

What is your honest view of the enemy?

How do you see yourself as being used in the overcoming of the kingdom of darkness and the spreading of the Kingdom of God? What are some battles in which you have faced the enemy and won?

What do you see as your strengths in being victorious when the enemy comes against you?

FURTHER READING

1 John 4:4

Luke 10:19

Ephesians 6:1-20

Ecclesiastes 4:12

PRAYER HELP: Journaling

We were college-age young adults on fire with the Holy Spirit, sitting at the feet of Deacon Joe Lessard, a masterful Bible teacher. Joe told us to turn to Acts 29. The pages started turning, and they turned, and they turned. Someone raised his hand and with a confused tone stated, *"Joe, I don't have Acts 29 in my Bible."* We all were in agreement. Joe went on to say to say that the Acts of the Apostles is the story of the Holy Spirit moving in the lives of the apostles and that the Acts of the Apostles had 28 chapters. Our lives were to be Acts 29.

I took this literally and started to keep, even more carefully, a record of my life in the Lord, using my journal. My journal is my Acts 29. It is the record of the Holy Spirit moving in my life. I keep that record as a testimony for my children's children and generations of other believers.

My journal is also the place where I pray at the point of a pen. Most of the time, this is what it looks like when I pray. Before me I have my Bible, pen and my journal. I write out my conversation with the Lord, recording what I say to him and what he says to me. I am praying at the point of my pen. This helps me to keep focused and it records what he is saying to me.

Another way to journal is to put down those things which will jog your memory as to what happened during your time of prayer. These entries do not need to be detailed or complete sentences. They might even be drawings. To others, what is entered might not make sense, but to you they bring to your memory all you need to see about what he was saying.

Over the years, through one journal after another, I have come to see that God speaks in puzzle pieces. He gives a little at a time. But when seen together, it makes sense. Most of us see a piece of what he says as isolated and without connection. To help with this, I begin every journal with an index. On the first five pages, I do not write. Then on page six, I begin numbering my pages so that page six is page one. At the end of my prayer and journaling time, I ask the Holy Spirit to summarize in a few words, my time with the Lord. In the index, I write the summary and the pages on which I have written. On Sunday, I review my index to look for a thread of what God is saying to tie all together. Then, on the first Friday I review my index to see if there is a greater thread. In this way, my journal becomes a place in which I can see the hand of God writing in my life.

DAY
TWENTY-EIGHT

Day 28: Ask for Workers

Then he said to his disciples, "The harvest is plentiful but the workers are few. Ask the Lord of the harvest, therefore, to send out workers into his harvest field." Matthew 9:37-38

MEDITATION

"You are my teacher." This is the greatest compliment I have ever received in my life because it came from my wife Andrea, before we were married. What joy fills my heart to know that grace allowed me to lead her to Jesus and form her in the ways of the Kingdom. I am her teacher and for this I am grateful to my *AhDah,* my Father. I was blessed to be with Andrea, her family, and 26 others in a Christian community which I oversaw and was the principal teacher. Another similar compliment with great weight was from my friend, Rob. He once wrote in my birthday card, *"Thank you for introducing me to your best friend. He is now mine."* In this, he was speaking of Jesus. I will never forget reading Rob's card and being reduced to tears of appreciation for the grace to share Jesus with others. To this day, I have that card. Rob put in words the purpose of my life. Jesus is my everything and I want everyone to know him.

Disciple of Jesus, for what higher cause is your life if it is not to help people become believers and then form them as disciples so that they too, might lead others to Christ? I am a worker in the harvest field, no matter the cost. Disciple, do you see yourself as a harvester, ready to do all you can to win souls to Jesus, whether it is comfortable or not, whether it suits your personality or not? Our hearts must cry, *"Souls! Souls! Souls!"* We must hunger, we must thirst, we must long, we must plan, we must plot for souls to come to Christ. Jesus, Jesus, Jesus is he for whom we must live and we must hope for other believers to do the same.

When one becomes an accountant, he becomes an accountant for himself. He does not become an accountant so that others will become accountants. When one becomes a salesman, a cashier, a customer service rep, a whatever it may be that one becomes, it is done for self. When one is a disciple, it is so that he might make disciples of others which will allow for the Kingdom of God to migrate from soul to soul to soul, through generation to generation to generation, from nation to nation to nation. Those of the Kingdom have found the pearl of great price and are willing to sell all that they must to possess that pearl and then they go off to share the wealth of that pearl with others.

The point is this – we are here to evangelize. It is the primary purpose of the Church and the primary action of the disciple.

With the bringing of souls to Jesus as our focus, our prayer should also be toward this end. We should pray in the spirit that sons and daughters of God be given the words they need to lead others to Jesus as Savior and Lord. I will be so bold as to say that there is a litmus test to see if a soul's heart is taken and captured by Jesus. Does that soul long for others to find what it has found? Does that soul believe that it has discovered that for which every heart is longing?

Let us not be confused by the lies of the flesh which falsely proclaim that the Kingdom spreads because of certain outgoing charismatic personalities who lead souls to Christ. This is a deception of the enemy for in it he causes certain believers, if not most, to accept as true the falsehood that they do not have what is needed to lead others to Jesus. What is necessary is followers of Jesus praying for each other, workers in the harvest, to be given anointed words by the Holy Spirit. It is not the cunning or skill of man that brings forth conversion, but the work of the Spirit of Truth, which calls to each soul in a way that the soul can hear that it is loved and desired by the Caller.

In school, whether high school or college, I was always blessed to be in honors English, not because I can diagram a sentence, but because I have always been able to express myself well through speech and writing. My senior year, I was assigned AP English. On the first day of class, I noticed that all the other students were freshmen. That was a day of grace. Though later, I found that I was in the wrong room. Above the chalk board, to the right, just before the clock, was a poster of a cookie cutter man made of other cookie cutter men. At the bottom, it read,

"I stand where I stand, now, because I stand on the shoulders of giants." Sir Isaac Newton

Though I left the room in embarrassment, the truth of that poster was etched on my heart and worth the price. I do not take lightly those who pray as I go forth with proclamation and demonstration of the Kingdom. It is on these shoulders I stand. Thank you! You Disciple, through your prayer, are shoulders on which others may stand to make known the mystery of the Gospel. In the Kingdom, there are two types: the one who proclaims the Gospel and the one who prays for the one who proclaims. In the *School of Prayer,* it is a given that all who call themselves disciples are to pray for workers to bring forth the harvest.

St. Paul says that we are to pray in the Spirit to intercede for those who are going forth with proclamation. Here, he is speaking of the gift of praying in tongues. Given that each soul is a mystery, we cannot imagine what grace that soul needs to surrender to Jesus. The beauty of the gift of tongues is that we do not need to understand. We need to allow the Spirit to do the praying through us so that the person speaking will have the anointed words for the listeners.

O Disciple, be you before the crowds or hidden in a forgotten home, you are not hidden from the work of the Kingdom. Today, pray in the Spirit, intercede for the harvesters that they may gather in a crop whose yield is more than can be imagined.

PRAYER

Father, Lord of the Harvest,
send forth workers into the field to gather to you soul upon soul. You desire that none be lost, that all would be saved. But how will they believe unless one is sent?
Jesus,
save souls!
Holy Spirit,
give me a hunger for souls and a burning drive to pray for you to send harvesters and to pray for those harvesters.
In Jesus' name.
Amen

ACTION

- Make a list of persons for whom you need to pray to come to Jesus and then pray for the persons who will evangelize those on your list. If you have the gift of tongues, use it for this purpose.
- With whom and what will you share from today's lesson?

REFLECTION QUESTIONS

Who do you know that has a gifting for ministry whom you could encourage to become involved in some work of the Kingdom?

How do you feel about your sharing the Gospel with someone?

136

With whom could you share the Gospel and for what should you pray before you share it?

What does this mean to you? *"Some give by going, while others go by giving?"*

FURTHER READING

Matthew 13:44-46

Matthew 10:19-20

Ephesians 6:19-20

Romans 10:13-15

1 Timothy 2:4

Day 29: Constant Schooling

If you remain in me and my words remain in you, ask whatever you wish, and it will be given you. John 15:7

MEDITATION

I love being a dad. I especially love babies and toddlers. A sad day for me is when I am dressing one of my little ones and they reach out to put their arms into the sleeves. That is a day of moving toward independence. The silliest thing is when they go to crawl, they are on all fours and they start rocking back and forth and many times they go backwards. It's fun to watch them walk along the couch and then the day comes when they step out into open space. Early childhood is one adventure after another, with one new skill acquired after another.

If a child is wedged in a stage, for example, never walking without holding onto something, it is called *protracted infancy*. This is not a healthy sign and later on will require help for the child. We would all agree that we would hope this would not happen to our children. If you face this with your child, know that as I write, I am praying for your child to be healed.

Disciple of Jesus, this is the truth for many in their spiritual lives. They are facing a *protracted spiritual infancy*. By this, I mean, they are praying the same way they did as a child, not progressing in spiritual maturity with the passing years. What a sad and abnormal state for their souls. Even more tragic is that they do not see that they are stunted and neither do the people around them, so they continue to grow in body but are underdeveloped in spirit. The work of the Holy Spirit is to take us from glory to glory. If, with the passing of the years, our spiritual life is not going deeper and deeper, causing us to be more like Jesus, then we have stagnated and eternal life is not growing within us.

In the *School of Prayer,* we are called to remain in Jesus and his word. As we abide in Jesus and in his word, we are transformed, growing, more and more into his image. We are not satisfied to be where we were yesterday. With each day, we are hungering for more of his presence and power in our life. Our heart's yearning must be,

"More, Jesus, more! I want more of you and more of your ways."

Each day, we are invited to enroll, anew, in his *School of Prayer,* beseeching, *"Lord, teach me to pray,"* with our heart desiring the new lesson his Spirit is craving to teach. Do not settle for the lesser, O Saint of God, when he stands with full hands to give you the greater. How many a soul has slipped from a soaring height in his presence to the mediocrity of the masses! Let this not be you, *Abba's* Son, *Abba's* Daughter. Your Father's dream for you is more than the place in which you are living. Abide in Jesus and in his word. Let this become not something you do, but your style of life. Dream with him into an ever-greater expansion of your spirited-soul. Every spiritual blessing is yours in the heavenlies through Christ Jesus. Every blessing is yours! Draw these graces to yourself and live from them, ever growing to become more like him.

Here are some ways you can continue to grow in *The School of Prayer* by remaining in Jesus and his in word:

- Commit to Sunday Mass and, if available, weekly adoration of the Blessed Sacrament.
- Find and commit to a Charismatic Prayer Group or join a Charismatic Covenant Community. If there are none in your area contact our ministry and we can come and help you build a Community of Disciples on Mission.
- Subscribe to *One Bread, One Body*, a free daily email based on the readings of the Mass. This tool will help you to remain in the Word.
- Download the app *Pray as You Go*. Again, this is based on the daily readings of the Mass with sacred music, one of the readings is proclaimed, and reflection questions are drawn from the given reading.
- Seek out someone who you know is mature in the spiritual life and ask this person to teach you from experience.
- At least once a year, attend a retreat, parish mission, or Church conference.
- Grow in hearing God's voice and follow his promptings. As you do so, more and more promptings will come your way, causing you to be conformed to his will in every moment.

Recently, I was asked by someone what I liked to do. I told him that I like to spend time with my wife. To this he further questioned, *"I mean, what type of hobbies do you have?"* My answer was the same. Because I am in love with Andrea and she with me I can think of no better way to spend my time. By us being together, more and more of her soul opens to me. Not that she has hidden anything, it is just that I am drawn by the chords of love further into the mystery of who she is. I cannot give enough of myself to her and I cannot receive enough of her into myself. On the second day of *The School of Prayer*, as we sat with the One whom our soul loves, we learned

"Prayer is not what you do. It is who you are with."

Continually nurture, grow, and deepen in the *School of Prayer*. Much more is about to open to you as you further study the life of prayer. You will learn the way of this Saint and the way of that one. Great teachers will suggest this method and others will offer you another. Soul of *Yahweh*, your *Abba*, always have this vision before the eyes of your heart - long to draw closer to him. Hunger for your time to be consumed with him present to you and you present to him. Heart whose flame is growing brighter and brighter with the kindling of desire, let not peace or joy be your goal, nor let it be bliss or personal fulfillment, for these are byproducts and not the essence for which you were made. You, beloved of Jesus, are made for him and he is burning with passion to give himself to you. Any other aspiration than the giving of yourself in total surrender and abandonment to him and you being filled with the fullness of him is too small for you. Do not settle for less, O soul for which he gave his Son. Have him and possess him, that he might have and possess you. It is this of which he dreams.

ACTION

- In your journal, write out a plan for you to grow to the next level of glory in your spiritual life.
- With whom and what will you share from today's lesson?

REFLECTION QUESTIONS

At what stage would you say you are in your spiritual life and why do you see yourself at that stage?

With whom could you partner and begin to pray together?

What are some things which you have learned from *The Disciple's School of Prayer*?

140

In what ways has *The Disciple's School of Prayer* helped you to grow in your spiritual life?

FURTHER READING

2 Corinthians 3:18

Proverbs 4:18

1 John 2:27

Matthew 18:20

Day 30: The Size of Faith

He replied, "Because you have so little faith. Truly I tell you, if you have faith as small as a mustard seed, you can say to this mountain, 'Move from here to there,' and it will move. Nothing will be impossible for you." Matthew 17:20

MEDITATION

I remember the first time I heard the Parable of the Mustard Seed. I was 15 years old and just had started attending Mass on a weekly basis. The Gospel was proclaimed and the priest began to preach. He held out his clenched thumb and index finger and told us that he was holding a mustard seed. It was so small that none of us could see it. At that point, I began to get excited. Jesus said that if I had faith the size of that which Father was holding and I could not see, I could say, *(fill in the blank),* and it was done. I wanted to shout out,

"I have faith that is bigger than the mustard seed. I believe bread and wine become Jesus' body and blood. We all have huge faith!"

I was a good boy. I sat there quietly. From that day forward I decided to be grateful for the abundant measure of faith which I have been given by my *AhDah.*

Disciple of Jesus, as we close this *School of Prayer*, I want to leave you with encouragement as to the magnitude of your faith. Here is how significantly blessed you are in faith. As you read, do not discount how blessed you are to believe such things.

- You believe that God became man and that Jesus is the God-Man. This takes great faith to look at a finite man and know that he is the infinite God. You have great faith!
- You believe that Jesus died for your sins and the sins of all and it is by faith in the power of his spilled blood that your sins and all sins can be forgiven. You have great faith!
- You believe that Jesus was dead and then rose from the dead on the third day. You believe in a dead man come back to life, conquering the grave. This is great faith!
- You believe that bread and wine, through the priesthood, become the body, blood, soul, and divinity of Jesus -- that it is no

longer bread, but it has become his Real Presence, which compels you to kneel down and worship. This is great faith!

Because of your great faith, disciple of Jesus, imagine all the Father wants to do in you and through you for the sake of the Kingdom. Imagine all the lives he will change for eternity through you. Could your hands have within them healing for a mom with five children dying of cancer? Hidden soul in the heart of Jesus, could the time you spend on your knees give words to those speaking to the lost to lead those souls to Jesus? It may well be, soul conformed to his Son, that the moments you spend with Jesus so transform your heart to love like him, that when a soul so broken by others becomes your friend, they find in you the love for which they have searched for their entire life. See with me, disciple of Jesus, a family in distress with an empty fridge and an eviction notice and you paying their bills, knowing that your *Abba* will supply your needs because you have been generous like him. Do not underestimate the authority you have, apostle of hope, to be able to speak to those bound by demons and set them free. And do not underestimate the effect their freedom will have on others.

Many times we are waiting on heaven to do something when heaven is waiting on us. I will never forget the experience of being a Eucharistic Visitor when I was 18 years old. I was assigned a nursing home. One day I gave Our Lord to an elderly woman who was wheelchair bound. After she communed, as I was kneeling next to her with my hand on the armrest of her chair, her skinny, bony hands began to tap on my hand. As she did so I looked at her and she stared intensely into my eyes and said, *"You are the answer to the prayers of many."* Even as I write, that memory is present to me. Disciple, by his grace and to his glory, we have mustard size faith and Jesus is sending us out to a broken world with the Kingdom of God in our hands. Call out to them,

"Look this way!
What you have spent your time pursuing has left you empty.
Let it go and come this way. (This is another way of saying, "Repent.")
Here in my hands, it is that close, is everything for which you have
      ever longed or desired.
Here is all the love for which your heart was made.
Here is the forgiveness you need for all you have done to hurt God,
      others, and yourself.
Here is your healing.
Here is your freedom from all the ways the enemy is holding you
      bound.
Here it is.
The price has been paid with the blood of Jesus and it is free to you.

Here is the Kingdom of God.
It is yours.
Take it!

Disciple of Jesus, we may never meet in this life, so let us live righteously to see each other in the Kingdom. And may we bring many with us. I look forward to meeting you, my brother, my sister of *Abba*, our Father. Let us love, no matter the cost.

PRAYER

Father, whose hands are filled with blessings,
thank you for the gift of faith.
You have given me greater than mustard seed size faith and I will use it for your glory.
Jesus,
here I am.
Send me.
Use me.
Holy Spirit,
teach me to pray.
Give me the grace to love the unlovable and to forgive the unforgivable.
The Kingdom is in my hands and I will give it to all.
In Jesus' name.
Amen

ACTION

- Keep your heart sensitive to the prompting of the Holy Spirit to share Jesus with others, even if it is uncomfortable.
- With whom and what will you share from today's lesson?

REFLECTION QUESTIONS

What do you believe about God that is astonishing?

Do you believe that you have mustard seed size faith or bigger?

144

What is an amazing act of grace with which you would like God to use you for others?

What do you think would help you to step into greater measures of faith in who God is and what he wants to do?

FURTHER READING

Matthew 4:19

Mark 16:15-20

John 14:12

2 Thessalonians 1:3-4

Appendix: Prayer methods

MORNING PRAYER TIME

For your morning prayer time, you might need to set the alarm and wake before your usual waking time. This is a worthy sacrifice which will hold out rewards in this life and the next.

Basic 15-minute Morning Prayer:

- In just a few words, ask the Holy Spirit to help you to pray.
- In some way give praise to God. (My book *Manual of Praise* could be helpful).
- Renew your baptismal vows by giving Him your life and professing that Jesus is Lord of your life and your day. You can also use the Morning Offering,
- Read a portion of the Word of God. The Gospels are always our priority.
- Spend a few minutes thinking about what you read.
- The monks always include the *Benedictus*, the Song of Zachariah, (Luke 1:68-79) which is a song of praise, to start their day.
- Intercessions for the upcoming day.
- End with the *Our Father*.

EVENING PRAYER

Evening prayer is a great time to look back at your day to see the presence and blessing of God and give Him thanks. Depending on your family needs, you might consider a time of prayer right after the dinner dishes are washed. If you are worn from the day, keep the prayer as basic as possible.

Basic 15-minute Evening Prayer:

- In just a few words, ask the Holy Spirit to help you to pray. (My book *Manual of Praise* could be helpful).
- In some way give praise to God.
- Review your day. Give thanks to God for the people and blessings you encountered.
- Re-read the portion of the Word of God you read in the morning. This will solidify it in your heart and mind.

- Spend a few minutes thinking about what you read and the thoughts that came to you throughout the day.
- The monks always include the *Magnificat*, Our Lady's Song of Praise (Luke 1:46-55), to end the day to give thanks for the blessings they have received.
- On reviewing the day, offer any intercessions which have arisen.
- End with the *Our Father.*

NIGHT PRAYER

I do not recommend that you lie down when you pray as you might drift off to sleep. This prayer does not need to be as long as morning and evening prayer.

<u>Basic Night Prayer</u>

- In just a few words, ask the Holy Spirit to help you to pray, specifically seeking the grace of repentance.
- Quickly review your day. Is there anyone you need to forgive and is there anything for which you did that you need forgiveness? Repent!
- The monks always include the *Nunc Dimittis*, the Prayer of Simeon (Luke 2:29-32), which is a prayer to give thanks to God for knowing Jesus and committing our soul to the Father's care.
- Pray the *Our Father.*
- Bless yourself and go to bed in peace!

MORNING OFFERING (Used at the Beginning of the Day)

O Jesus, through the Immaculate Heart of Mary, I offer You my prayers, works, joys and sufferings of this day for all the intentions of Your Sacred Heart, in union with the Holy Sacrifice of the Mass throughout the world, in reparation for my sins, for the poor souls in purgatory, the reunion of all Christians, and in particular for the intentions of our Holy Father for this month.

DAILY LIFE REVIEW (Used in Evening or Before Bed)

Come Holy Spirit, fill the hearts of Thy faithful and enkindle in them the fire of Thy love. Send forth Thy Spirit and they shall be created. And Thou shalt renew the face of the earth.

Rejoice - Look back at your day and thank God for the blessings.

Release - As an act of your will, forgive anyone that has offended you, be it great or small.

Repent - Let the Holy Spirit search your heart for sin.

Rebuke - If you have let the enemy have any control, break his power in Jesus name.

Request - Ask for your needs that you have become aware of through the day.

Resolve - As you review your day, exercise your will to be conformed more closely to God's will.

LITURGY OF THE HOURS or DIVINE OFFICE

Under the old covenant, a sacrifice was offered every morning at 9am and every evening at 3pm. As the priests were preparing and offering the lamb, the people of God would gather in the outer court of the Temple and chant the psalms. Jews, at the time of Jesus, saw the Book of Psalms as the prayer book of Israel and would have memorized all 150 psalms and used these psalms during the many prayer celebrations, sacrifices, and festivals of Israel. We read in the Book of Acts 3:1 of Peter and John going up to the Temple for the evening sacrifice. We are a priestly people (1 Peter 2:9) and as such are to offer God the sacrifice of praise. The early Church, as evidenced by Peter and John, continued to pray the psalms. That tradition has been handed down to this day. In the monastery, the brothers will gather for the Liturgy of the Hours, eight times in a day:

Office of Readings (12 midnight or 3am)
Morning Prayer (6am)
Midmorning Prayer (9am)
Noon Prayer (12 noon)
Midafternoon Prayer (3pm)
Evening prayer (6pm)
Night Prayer (9pm)

In the monastery, the way of life is that of *Ora et Labora*, prayer and work. The rhythm of the day is divided between praying the Word, then work, as one meditates on the Word, to return to pray the Word. In this way prayer is brought into work and work is brought into prayer and time is sanctified. Imagine your life lived by this rhythm and the great blessing that this rhythm would bring to seeing God in your *"everydayness"* of life.

Below, I have laid forth the foundation times of the Hours, Morning and Evening Prayer. You can buy books for the Liturgy of the Hours, but what I have done is made it so you can pray from your Bible. It should be noted that you will need a Bible with all the books and not one in which

148

seven of the books have been removed. The Bible you will need is commonly called a *Catholic Bible*.

Flow of Morning and Evening Prayer

1) "God come to my assistance. Lord, make haste to help me."
2) 3 Psalms or Canticle, before and after which an antiphon which is *italicized* is prayed and then followed by the Glory to...
3) Reading (In parenthesis following the Name of the Day and is Bold. Please refer to pages 147 and following for readings.)
4) In the Morning - Canticle of Zechariah / *Benedictus* (Lk 1:68-79)
   In the Evening – Canticle of Mary / *Magnificat* (Lk 1:46-55)
5) Intercessions
6) Our Father
7) Closing Prayer

Glory to

Glory to the Father, and to the Son, and to the Holy Spirit;
As it was in the beginning, is now, and will be forever.

Morning - Canticle of Zechariah / Benedictus

Blessed be the Lord, the God of Israel;
he has come to his people and set them free.
He has raised up for us a mighty savior,
born of the house of his servant David.
Through his holy prophets he promised of old
that he would save us from our enemies,
from the hands of all who hate us.
He promised to show mercy to our fathers
and to remember his holy covenant.
This was the oath he swore
to our father Abraham:
to set us free from the hands of our enemies,
free to worship him without fear,
holy and righteous in his sight
all the days of our life.
You, my child, shall be called the prophet
of the Most High;
for you will go before the Lord
to prepare his way,
to give his people knowledge of salvation
by the forgiveness of their sins.
In the tender compassion of our God
the dawn from on high shall break upon us,

149

to shine on those who dwell in darkness
and the shadow of death.
and to guide our feet into the way of peace.

Glory to the Father, and to the Son,
and to the Holy Spirit,
as it was in the beginning, is now,
and will be forever. Amen.

Evening – Canticle of Mary / Magnificat

My soul proclaims the greatness of the Lord,
my spirit rejoices in God my Savior
for he has looked with favor
on his lowly servant.
From this day, all generations
will call me blessed:
the Almighty has done great things for me,
and holy is his Name.
He has mercy on those who fear him
in every generation.
He has shown the strength of his arm,
he has scattered the proud in their conceit.
He has cast down the mighty
from their thrones,
and has lifted up the lowly.
He has filled the hungry with good things,
and the rich he has sent away empty.
He has come to the help of his servant Israel
for he has remembered his promise of mercy,
the promise he made to our fathers,
to Abraham and his children forever.

Glory to the Father, and to the Son,
and to the Holy Spirit,
as it was in the beginning, is now,
and will be forever. Amen.

Week I
Sunday, Evening (Romans 11:33-36)
Ps 141:1-9 *Like burning incense, Lord, let my prayer rise up to you.*
Ps 142 *You are my refuge, Lord; you are all I desire in life.*
Phil 2:6-11 *The Lord Jesus humbled himself, and God exalted him forever.*

Sunday, Morning (Rev 7:10, 12)
Ps 63:2-9 *As morning breaks I look to you, O God, to be my strength this day, Alleluia!*
Dan 3:57-88, 56 *From the midst of the flame the three young men cried out with one voice: Blessed be God, Alleluia!*
Ps 149 *Let the people of Zion rejoice in their king, Alleluia!*
Sunday, Evening (2 Cor 1:3-4)
Ps 110:1-5,7 *The Lord will stretch forth his mighty scepter from Zion, and will reign forever, Alleluia!*
Ps 114: *The earth is shaken to its depths before the glory of your face.*
Rev 19:1-7 *All power is yours, Lord God, our mighty King, Alleluia!*

Monday, Morning (2 Thess 3:10b-13)
Ps 5:2-10, 12-13 *I lift up my heart to you, O Lord, and you will hear my morning prayer.*
1 Chr 29:10-13 *We praise your glorious name, O Lord, our God.*
Ps 29 *Adore the Lord in his holy court.*
Monday, Evening (Col 1:9b-11)
Ps 11 *The Lord looks tenderly on those who are poor.*
Ps 15 *Blessed are the poor of heart, for they shall see God.*
Eph 1:3-10 *God chose us in his Son to be his adopted children.*

Tuesday, Morning (Rm 13:11b,12-13a)
Ps 24 *The man whose deeds are blameless and whose heart is pure will climb the mountain of the Lord.*
Tb 13:1-8 *Praise the eternal King in all your deeds.*
Ps 33 *The loyal heart must praise the Lord.*
Tuesday, Evening (1 Jn 3:1a,2)
Ps 20 *God has crowned his Christ with victory.*
Ps 21:2-8, 14 *We celebrate your mighty works with songs of praise, Lord.*
Rev 4:11; 5:9,10,12 *Lord, you have made us a kingdom and priest for God our Father*

Wednesday, Morning (Tob 4:15a, 16a, 18a, 19)
Ps 36 *O Lord, in your light we see light itself.*
Jud 16:2-3a,13-15 *O God, you are great and glorious; we marvel at your power.*
Ps 47 *Exult in God's presence with hymns of praise.*
Wednesday, Evening (Jm 1:22,25)
Ps 27:1-6 *The Lord is my light and my help, whom shall?*
Ps 27:7-14 *I long to look no you; do not turn your face from me.*
Col 1:12-20 *He is the first-born of all creation; in every way primacy is his.*

Thursday, Morning (Is 66:1-2)

Ps 57 *Awake, lyre and harp, with praise let us awake the dawn.*
Jer 31:10-14 *My people, says the Lord, will be filled with my blessing.*
Ps 48 *The Lord is great and worthy to be praised in the city of our God.*
Thursday, Evening (1 Pt 1:6-9)
Ps 30 *I cried to you, Lord, and you healed me; I will praise you forever.*
Ps 32 *The one who is sinless in the eyes of God is blessed indeed.*
Rev 11:17-18,; 12:10b12a *The Father has given Christ all power, honor and kingship; all people will obey him.*

Friday, Morning (Eph 4:49-32)
Ps 51 *Lord, you will accept the true sacrifice offered on your altar.*
Is 45:15-25 *All descendants of Israel will glory in the Lord's gift of victory.*
Ps 100 *Let us go into God's presence singing for joy.*
Friday Evening (Rm 15:1-3)
Ps 41 *Lord lay your healing hand upon me, for I have sinned.*
Ps 46 *The mighty Lord is with us; the God of Jacob is our stronghold.*
Rev 15:3-4 *All nations will come and worship before you, O Lord.*

Saturday, Morning (2 Pt 1:10-11)
Ps 119:145-152 *Dawn finds me ready to welcome you, my God.*
Ex 15:1-4a, 8-13, 17-18 *The Lord is my strength, and I shall sing his praise, for he has become my Savior.*
Ps 117 *O praise the Lord, all you nations.*

Week II
Sunday, Evening (Col 1:2b-6a)
Ps 119:105-112 *Your word, O Lord, is the lantern to light our way, Alleluia.*
Ps 16 *When I see your face, O Lord, I shall know the fullness of joy, Alleluia.*
Phil 2:6-11 *Let everything in heaven and on the earth, bend the knee at the name of Jesus, Alleluia.*
Sunday, Morning (Ez 36:25-27)
Ps 118 *Blessed is he who comes in the name of the Lord, Alleluia.*
Dan 3:52-57 *Let us sing a hymn of praise to God, Alleluia.*
Ps 150 *Praise the Lord for his infinite greatness, Alleluia.*
Sunday, Evening (2 Thess 2:13-14)
Ps 110:1-5,7 *Christ our Lord is a priest forever, like Melchizedek of old, Alleluia.*
Ps 115 *God dwells in highest heaven; he has power to do all he wills, Alleluia.*
Rev 19:1-7 *Praise God, all you who serve him, both great and small, Alleluia.*

Monday, Morning (Jer 15:16)
Ps 42 *When will I come to the end of my pilgrimage and enter the presence of God.*
Sir 36:1-5,10-13 *Lord, show us the radiance of your mercy.*
Ps 19:1-7 *The vaults of heaven ring out your praise, O Lord.*
Monday, Evening (1 Thess 2:13)
Ps 45:1-10 *Yours is more than mortal beauty; every word you speak is full of grace.*
Ps 45:11-18 *The Bridegroom is here; go out and welcome him.*
Eph 1:3-10 *God planned in the fullness of time to restore all things in Christ*

Tuesday, Morning (1 Thess 5:4-5)
Ps 43 *Lord, send forth your light and your truth.*
Is 38:10-14,17-20 *Lord, keep us safe all the days of our life.*
Ps 65 *To you, O God, our praise is due in Zion.*
Tuesday, Evening (Rom 3:23-25a)
Ps 49:1-13 *You cannot serve both god and mammon.*
Ps 49:14-21 *Store up for yourself treasures in heaven, says the Lord.*
Rev 4:11; 5:9,10,12 *Adoration and glory belong by right to the Lamb that was slain.*

Wednesday, Morning (Rom 8:35,37)
Ps 77 *O God, all your ways are holy; what god can compare with our God.*
1 Sam 2:1-10 *My heart leaps with joy to the Lord, for he humbles only to exalt.*
Ps 96 *The Lord is king, let the earth rejoice.*
Wednesday, Evening (1Pt 5:5b-7)
Ps 62 *Eagerly we await the fulfillment of our hope, the glorious coming of our Savior.*
Ps 67 *May God turn his radiant face towards us and fill us with his blessing.*
Col 1:12-20 *Through him all things were made; he holds all creation together in himself.*

Thursday, Morning (Rom 14:17-19)
Ps 80 *Stir up your mighty power, Lord; come to our aid.*
Is 12:1-6 *The Lord has worked marvels for us; make it known to the ends of the earth.*
Ps 81 *Ring out your joy to God our strength.*
Thursday, Evening (1 Pt 1:22-23)
Ps 72:1-11 *I have made you a light of all nations to carry my salvation to the ends of the earth.*

Ps 72:12-19 *The Lord will save the children of the poor and rescue them from slavery.*
Rev 11:17-18; 12:10b-12a *Now the victorious reign of our God has begun.*

Friday, Morning (Eph 2:13-16)
Ps 51 *A humble, contrite heart, O God, you will not spurn.*
Hab 3:2-4, 13a, 15-19 *Even in your anger, Lord, you will remember compassion.*
Ps 147:12-20 *O praise the Lord, Jerusalem!*
Friday Evening (1 Cor 2:7-10a)
Ps 116:1-9 *Lord, keep my soul from death, never let me stumble.*
Ps 121 *My help comes from the Lord, who made heaven and earth.*
Rev 15:3-4 *King of all ages, your ways are perfect and true.*

Saturday, Morning (Rom 12:14-16a)
Ps 92 *As morning breaks we sing of your mercy, Lord, and nights finds us proclaiming your fidelity.*
Deut 32:1-12 *Extol the greatness of our God.*
Ps 8 *How wonderful is your name, O Lord, in all creation.*

Week III
Sunday, Evening (Heb 13:20-21)
Ps 113 *Rejoice, Jerusalem, let your joy overflow, your Savior will come to you, Alleluia!*
Ps 116:10-19 *I shall take into my hand the saving chalice and invoke the name of the Lord.*
Phil 2:6-11 *The Lord Jesus humbled himself, and God exalted him.*
Sunday, Morning (Ez 37:12b-14)
Ps 93 *Glorious is the Lord on high, Alleluia!*
Dan 3:57-88,56 *To you, Lord, be highest glory and praise for ever, Alleluia!*
Ps 148 *Praise the Lord from the heavens, Alleluia!*
Sunday, Evening (1 Pt 1:3-5)
Ps 110:1-5,7 *The Lord said to my Master: Sit at my right hand, Alleluia!*
Ps 111 *Our compassionate Lord has left us a memorial of his wonderful work, Alleluia!*
Rev 19:1-7 *All power is yours, Lord God, our mighty King, Alleluia!*

Monday, Morning (Jm 2:12-13)
Ps 84 *Blessed are they who dwell in your house, O Lord.*
Is 2:2-5 *Come, let us climb the mountain of the Lord.*
Ps 96 *Sing to the Lord and bless his name.*
Monday, Evening (Jm 4:11-12)

Ps 123 *Our eyes are fixed intently on the Lord, waiting for his merciful help.*

Ps 124 *Our help is in the name of the Lord who made heaven and earth.*

Eph 1:3-10 *God chose us in his Son to be his adopted children.*

Tuesday, Morning (1 Jn 4:14-15)
Ps 85 *Lord, you have blessed your land; you have forgiven the sins of your people.*

Is 26:1-4,7-9,12 *My soul has yearned for you in the night, and as morning breaks I long for your coming.*

Ps 67 *Lord, let your face shine upon us.*

Tuesday, Evening (Ro 12:9-12)
Ps 125 *The Lord surrounds his people with strength.*

Ps 131 *Unless you acquire the heart of a child, you cannot enter the kingdom of God.*

Rev 4:11; 5:9, 10, 12 *Lord, you have made us a kingdom and priest for God our Father.*

Wednesday, Morning (Job 1:21; 2:10b)
Ps 86 *Give joy to your servant, Lord; to you I lift up my heart.*

Is 33:13-16 *Blessed is the upright man, who speaks the truth.*

Ps 98 *Let us celebrate with joy in the presence of our God and King.*

Wednesday, Evening (Eph 3:20-21)
Ps 126 *Those who sow in tears will reap in joy.*

Ps 127 *May the Lord build our house and guard our city.*

Col 1:12-20 *He is the first-born of all creation,; in every way the primacy is his.*

Thursday, Morning (1 Pt 4:10-11a)
Ps 87 *Glorious things are said of you, O city of God.*

Is 40:10-17 *The Lord, the mighty conqueror, will come; he will bring with him the prize of victory.*

Ps 99 *Give praise to the Lord, our God, bow down before his holy mountain.*

Thursday, Evening (1 Pt 3:8-9)
Ps 132:1-10 *Let your holy people rejoice, O Lord, as they enter your dwelling place.*

Ps 132: 11-18 *The Lord has chosen Zion as his sanctuary.*

Rev 11:17-18; 12:10b-12a *The Father has given Christ all power, honor and kingship; all people will obey him.*

Friday, Morning (2 Cor 12:9-10)
Ps 51 *You alone have I grieved by my sin; have pity on me, O Lord.*

Jer 14:17-21 *Truly we know our offenses, Lord, for we have sinned against you.*

Ps 100 *The Lord is God; we are His people, the flock he shepherds.*
Friday Evening (Js 1:2-4)
Ps 135:1-12 *Great is the Lord, our God, transcending all other gods.*
Ps 135:13-21 *House of Israel, bless the Lord! Sing psalms to him, for he is merciful.*
Rev 15:3-4 *All nations will come and worship before you, O Lord.*

Saturday, Morning (Phil 2:14-15)
Ps 119:145-152 *Lord, you are near to us, and all your ways are true.*
Wis 9:1-6,9-11 *Wisdom of God, be with me, always at work in me.*
Ps 117 *The Lord remains faithful to his promises forever.*

Week IV
Sunday, Morning (2 Tim 2:8, 11-13)
Ps 118 *Praise the Lord, for his loving kindness will never fail.*
Dan 3:52-57 *Alleluia! Bless the Lord, all you works of the Lord, Alleluia!*
Ps 150 *Let everything that breathes give praise to the Lord.*
Sunday, Evening (1 Pt 2:21-24)
Ps 110:1-5,7 *In eternal splendor, before the dawn on earth, I have begotten you, Alleluia!*
Ps 112 *Blessed are those who fear the LORD, who find great delight in his commands.*
Rev 19:1-7 *Praise God, all you who serve him, both great and small, Alleluia!*

Monday, Morning (Jd 8:25-27)
Ps 90 *Each morning Lord, fill us with your kindness.*
Is 42: 10-16 *From the farthest bounds of the earth, may God be praised.*
Ps 135:1-12 *You who stand in the sanctuary, praise the Lord.*
Monday, Evening (1 Thess 3:12-13)
Ps 136:1-9 *Give thanks to the Lord, for his great love is without end.*
Ps 136:10-26 *Great and wonderful are your deeds, Lord God the Almighty.*
Eph 1:3-10 *God planned in the fullness of time to restore all things in Christ.*

Tuesday, Morning (Is 55:1)
Ps 101 *I will sing to you, O Lord; I will learn from you the way of perfection.*
Dan 3:26-27,29,34-41 *Lord, do not withhold your compassion from us.*
Ps 144:1-10 *O God, I will sing to you a new song.*
Tuesday, Evening (Col 3:16)

Ps 137:1-6 *If I forget you Jerusalem, Let my right-hand wither.*
Ps 138 *In the presence of the angels I will sing to you, my God.*
Rev 4:11; 5:9, 10, 12 *Adoration and glory belong by right to the Lamb who was slain.*

Wednesday, Morning (Deut 4:39-40a)
Ps 108 *My heart is ready, O God, my heart is ready.*
Is 61:10-62:5 *The Lord has robed me with grace and salvation.*
Ps 146 *I will praise my God all the days of my life.*
Wednesday, Evening (1 Jn 2:3-6)
Ps 139:1-12 *Lord, how wonderful is your wisdom, so far beyond my understanding.*
Ps 139:13-18, 23-24 *I am the Lord: I search the mind and probe the heart; I give to each one as his deeds deserve.*
Col 1:12-20 *Through him all things were made; he holds all creation together in himself.*

Thursday, Morning (Ro 8:18-21)
Ps 1431-11 *At daybreak, be merciful to me, O Lord.*
Is 66:10-14a *The Lord will make a river of peace flow through Jerusalem.*
Ps 147:1-11 *Let us joyfully praise the Lord our God.*
Thursday, Evening (Col 1:23)
Ps 144:1-8 *He is my comfort and my refuge. In him I put my trust.*
Ps 144:9-15 *Blessed are the people whose God is the Lord.*
Rev 11:17-18; 12:10b-12a *Now the victorious reign of our God has begun.*

Friday, Morning (Gal 2:19b-20)
Ps 51 *Create a clean heart in me, O God; renew in me a steadfast spirit.*
Tob 13:8-11, 13-15 *Rejoice, Jerusalem, for through you all men will be gathered.*
Ps 147:12-20 *Zion, praise your God, who sent his word to renew the earth.*
Friday Evening (Ro 8:1-2)
Ps 145:1-13 *Day after day I will bless you, Lord; I will tell of your marvelous deeds.*
Ps 145:14-21 *To you alone, Lord, we look with confidence; you are close to those who call upon you.*
Rev 15:3-4 *King of all ages, your ways are perfect and true.*

Saturday, Morning (2 Pt 3:13-15a)
Ps 92 *We do well to sing to your name, Most High, and proclaim your mercy at day break.*

Ez 36:24-28 *I will create a new heart in you, and breathe into you a new spirit.*

Ps 8 *On the lips of children and infants you have found perfect praise.*

Flow of Morning and Evening Prayer

1) God, come to my assistance.
   Lord, make haste to help me.
2) A brief examination of conscience.
3) Psalm
4) Reading
5) Into your hands, Lord, I commend my spirit.
   You have redeemed us, Lord God, of truth.
   Glory to the Father ...
6) Into your hands, Lord, I commend my spirit.
7) Nunc Dimitus Luke 2:29-32.
   Protect us, Lord, as we stay awake; watch over us as we sleep, that awake we may keep watch with Christ, and asleep, rest in his peace.

   Lord, now you let your servant go in peace; your word has been fulfilled: my own eyes have seen the salvation which you have prepared in the sight of every people: a light to reveal you to the nations and the glory of your people Israel

   Protect us, Lord, as we stay awake; watch over us as we sleep, that awake, we may keep watch with Christ, and asleep, rest in his peace.
8) Closing Prayer

Sunday Night Prayer (Deut 6:4-7)
Ps 4 *Have mercy on me, Lord, and hear my prayer.*
Ps 134 *In the silent hours of the night, bless the Lord.*

Monday Night Prayer (1 Thess 5:9-10)
Ps 86 *O Lord, our God, unwearied is your love for us.*

Tuesday Night Prayer (1 Pt 5:8-9a)
Ps 134:1-11 *Do not hide your face from me; in you I put my trust.*

Wednesday Night Prayer (Eph 4:26-27)
Ps 31:1-6 *Lord God, be my refuge and strength.*

Thursday Night Prayer (1 Thess 5:23)

Pray the Psalms in 20 Days

Day	Morning	Evening	Night
I	Ps 1-3	Ps 4-6	Ps 7-8
II	Ps 9-11	Ps 12-14	Ps 15-17
III	Ps 18	Ps 19-21	Ps 22-24
IV	Ps 25-27	Ps 28-30	Ps 31-32
V	Ps 33-34	Ps 35-36	Ps 37
VI	Ps 38-39	Ps 40-42	Ps 43-46
VII	Ps 47-49	Ps 50-52	Ps 53-55
VIII	Ps 56-58	Ps 59-61	Ps 62-64
IX	Ps 65-67	Ps 68	Ps 69-70
X	Ps 71-72	Ps 73-74	Ps 75-77
XI	Ps 78-79	Ps 80-81	Ps 82-84
XII	Ps 85-88	Ps 89	Ps 90-91
XIII	Ps 92-94	Ps 95-97	Ps 98-101
XIV	Ps 102-103	Ps 104	Ps 105
XV	Ps 106	Ps 107	Ps 108-109
XVI	Ps 110-112	Ps 113-115	Ps 116-118
XVII	Ps119:1-72	Ps119:73-128	Ps119:129-176, Ps 120
XVIII	Ps 121-124	Ps 125-129	Ps 130-134
XIX	Ps 135-137	Ps 138-140	Ps 141-144
XX	Ps 145	Ps 146-147	Ps 148-150

Ignatian Contemplation

Ignatian contemplation is not to be confused with the traditional use of the word, contemplation, which implies a stillness. Ignatian contemplation is the sanctification and active use of the imagination by the prayerful reading of the Word of God. Here are the steps:

1. Declare your dependence on God.
2. Select a passage.
3. Based on what you have read, ask God for the grace that is presented through the Word you have encountered.
4. Read the story and become part of it as someone who is watching the story unfold: Hear the sounds; notice the characters in the story and their reactions; notice your reactions.
5. Ask yourself, "What difference should being here and witnessing this make in my life?"
6. If it is a Gospel Story, dialogue with Jesus about what you have experienced.
7. Journal about these thoughts or feelings.
8. Close with an "Our Father".

Passages to Contemplate

Lk 1:26-38	Mt 21:1-11	Lk 24:36-43
Lk 2:1-7	Lk 17:11-19	Lk 24:44-53
Jn 1:29-39	Mt 26:20-30	Jn 21:15-19
Mk 1:9-11	Jn 13:1-30	Jn 20:24-29
Lk 4:16-22	Mt 26:30-46	Mt 28:16-20
Mk 1:16-20	Mt 26:47-56	Acts 19:1-19
Mt 8:23-27	Mt 26:57-68	Acts 2:1-4
Mt 14:22-43	Mt 26:69-75	Acts 3:1-10
Jn 5:1-9	Mt 27:11-26	Acts 16:16-34
Lk 8:43-48	Mt 27:27-31	Rev 1:9-20
Lk 19:1-10	Jn 17-19	Rev 7:9-17
Jn 11:38-44	Jn 20:1-10	Rev 12:7-9
Lk 7:36-50	Mt 28:1-9	Rev 19:11-16
Mk 10:46-52	Jn 20:19-23	Rev 21:1-4
Mt 17:1-9	Jn 21:1-14	Rev 22:1-5
Mt 16:13-20	Lk 24:13-35	

Ignatian Meditation

The Ignatian method of prayerful meditation is to approach poetic and wisdom passages of scripture with a pondering heart. Here are the steps:

1. Declare your dependence on God.
2. Select a passage.
3. Based on what you have read, ask God for the grace presented through the Word you have encountered.
4. Read the passage slowly, aloud or in a whisper, letting each word be heard by your heart so as to saturate your soul.
5. Stay with the words that catch your attention. Absorb them the way the parched earth receives the rain.
6. Keep repeating the word or phrase as you are aware of the feelings that are awakened.
7. Read and reread the passage as if you would a letter from a dear friend, knowing that it is God, your Father, that has had the Word of God written for you.
8. Dialogue with Jesus, Mary, or one of the Saints regarding the passage.
9. Journal about these thoughts or feelings.
10. Close with an "Our Father".

Passages to Meditate Upon

Is 55	Mt 6:25-34	Gal 5:16-25
Hos 11:1-9	Lk 11:1-13	Eph 1:3-14
Is 43:1-7	Ps 106	Mi 6:8
Lk 12:22-31	Mt 13:4-23	Phil 3:5-13
Ps 139	Mt 18:21-35	Jer 29:4-14
Ps 63	Ez 16	Ex 33:12-16
1 Sam 3:1-19	2 Cor 12:7-10	Jos 1:3-9
Jn 3:22-36	Lk 15:11-32	Ps 91
Gen 22:1-18	Ps 51	Rom 8:28-39
Ps 104	Rom 8:1-13	Eph 5:1-2
Ps 105	Jn 15:1-12	Rom 5:7-11
Ps 136	Ez 36:20-36	1 Jn 3:1
Mt 5:1-16	Jer 31	
Lk 6:27-38	Heb 11-12	

Daily Confession of Faith

- This is the day the Lord has made. I will rejoice and be glad in it (Ps 118:24).
- I enter into this day confessing that you, Lord, my God, are one (Deut 6:4), A Trinity of persons:
- Father, Son, and Holy Spirit (Mat 28:19). You are the one, true, living God (1 Thess 1:9), besides whom there is no other (Is 45:6).
- I cry with all the heavenly host: "Holy, holy, holy is the Lord; who was and is and is to come" (Rev 4:8).
- This day I renew my baptism by rejecting sin and living for God in Christ Jesus (Ro 6:11)
- This day I refuse to be mastered by sin (Ro 6:14).
- This day it is my will to give no foothold to the devil (Eph 4:27). Rather, I believe in God, the Father, almighty, my Father, who is the maker of heaven and earth.
- I believe in Jesus Christ, my Lord, my Savior, who was born of the Virgin Mary, suffered under Pontius Pilot, was crucified, died and was buried; on the third day he rose again, and will come to judge the living and the dead. I believe in the Holy Spirit, the holy Catholic Church, the communion of saints, the forgiveness of sin, and life everlasting.
- This day, Lord, let your presence go with me (Ex 33:14), hem me in, before and behind (Ps 139: 5).
- In baptism, I have received the Holy Spirit (Ac 2:38), therefore, I cry out "Abba, Father" (Ro 8:15).
- Father, I seek first your kingdom (Mat 6:33). May your kingdom come and your will be done in my life (Mat 6:10).
- To walk in your will, I receive your guidance (Is 30:21) and your correction (Heb 12:6). I open my heart to your voice which is behind me saying, "This is the way, walk in it." (Is 30:21).
- I am not fearful, but I move in power, love, and self-control (2 Tim 1:6).
- I offer my life as a living sacrifice. This day, I will not be conformed to the world but I will be transformed by the renewing of my mind that I might choose what is your good, pleasing acceptable will (Rom 12:1-2).
- Jesus, you are my savior (Ac 4:12).
- Jesus, you are my Lord (Phil 2:1).
- You have bought me at the price of your blood (1 Cor 6:20).
- Because of you, Jesus, I have direct access to the Father (Heb 4:16).
- Because of you, Jesus, my sins are forgiven (Col 1:14), for your blood has cleansed me of all unrighteousness (1 Jn 1:7).
- Because of you, Jesus, there is no condemnation for me (Rom 8:1).
- Because of you, Jesus, I am seated in heavenly places (Eph 2:6).
- Because of you, Jesus, I have been given fullness (Col 2:10) and you will meet all my needs, this day, according to your glorious riches (Phil

4:19).

- Because of you, Jesus, this day, every spiritual blessing is mine (Eph 1:3).
- This day I know who I am and the mission to which I have been called, for in my baptism I was anointed and appointed to be priest, prophet and king.
- I am a priest, so this day I will worship the King and make intercession for all the needs of the Kingdom.
- I am a prophet, so this day I will teach all I meet the Gospel of the Kingdom.
- I am a king, so this day I will bring everything I say and do under the authority of the Kingdom of God.
- Today, Holy Spirit, increase my faith, strengthen my hope, and deepen my love (1 Cor 13:13).
- Holy Spirit, be my helper, abide in me, and lead me to all truth (Jn 14:16-17).
- I am your temple (1 Cor 6:19) and I am filled with you, Holy Spirit (Eph 5:18).
- I choose to abide in Christ (Jn 15:5), so I will bear the fruit of love, joy, peace, patience, kindness, generosity, faithfulness, gentleness, and self-control (Gal 5:25).
- Spirit of the living God, be sealed fresh in me (Eph 4:30) as on the day of my Confirmation and grant me fear of the Lord, piety, counsel, wisdom, fortitude, knowledge and understanding (Is 11:2-3) .
- For the sake of the building up of the body, the Church (1 Cor 12:7) I desire the spiritual gifts (1 Cor 14:1) and I desire an abundance of them in my life (1 Cor 14:12)
- I desire the word of knowledge, and the word of wisdom. I desire faith, healings, miracles, and prophecy. I desire discerning of spirits, tongues and interpretation of tongues (1 Cor 12:8-10).
- Use me to do your works as I ask in Jesus' name (Jn 14:12).
- Today, my love will be sincere (Ro 12:9) and I will love others as Christ has loved me (Jn 15:12).
- Today, if I am hurt or offended, knowingly or unknowingly, rightly or wrongly, I chose to forgive even as I have been forgiven (Col 3:13) and I ask forgiveness of anyone I will hurt or offend knowingly or unknowingly, rightly or wrongly. I will bless those who curse me, I will do good to those who hate me, and I will pray for those who despitefully use me (Mat 5:44).
- By these things I will do whatever needs to be done to make peace, thus I will demonstrate that I am a child of God (Mat 5:9).
- This day, I am not overcome by evil, but I overcome evil with good (Ro 12:21).
- This day I will not be lacking in zeal, but I will keep my spiritual fervor serving the Lord (Ro 12:11).

- I have been given freely, so freely will I give (Mt 10:8) and I will excel in my giving (2 Cor 8:7).
- This day I will share with all God's people who are in need (Rom 12:13).
- I do nothing out of selfish ambition, but I consider others better than myself (Phil 2:3).
- I am a servant (Matt 23:11).
- I will look for opportunities to practice the corporal acts of mercy by feeding the hungry, giving drink to the thirsty, clothing the naked, visiting the prisoner, sheltering the homeless, visiting the sick and burying the dead.
- I will also practices the spiritual works of mercy by admonishing the sinner, instructing the ignorant, counseling the doubtful, comforting the sorrowful, bearing all wrongs patiently, forgiving all injuries, and praying for the living and the dead.
- Today is set before me a blessing and a curse, life and death and I choose life that I might live (Deut 30:19), I choose the abundant life that Jesus came to bring me (Jn 10:10).
- I reject all negative emotions of fear, loneliness, anger, lust, greed, pride; I apply to the doorpost of my life and the lives of all my family and friends, the blood of the Lamb (Ex 12:13).
- I am strong in the Lord and the power of his might.
- I place on myself the armor of God that I may be able to stand against the wiles of the devil: I gird my loins with truth and have on the breastplace of righteousness. My feet are shod with readiness for the Gospel of peace. I take the shield of faith that I might extinguish the fiery darts of the wicked. I take the helmet of salvation and the sword of the Spirit which is the Word of God.
- I pray in the Spirit making supplication for all the saints and that utterance and boldness may given to all who open their mouths to make known the mystery of the Gospel (Eph 6:10-19).
- I submit to God and I resist the devil and he must flee (Jas 4:11).
- No weapon formed against me this day shall prosper (Is 54:17).
- In the name of Jesus I break every curse, hex and spell that has been uttered against me.
- This day every unclean spirit that would come against me I command to bend its knee to the name of Jesus (Phil 2:10). I proclaim a hedge of protection (Job 1:10) for myself, my family, my friends and the Church around our spiritual life, our health, our emotions, our finances, our relationships, our possessions, and our work. I defeat the devil, the accuser of the brethren by my testimony and the blood of the blood of the Lamb; and by not loving my life more than death (Rev 12:10-11).
- This day the boundaries have fallen in pleasant places for me (Ps 16:6).
- This day I am a child of God (1 Jn 3:1); I am a partaker of the divine nature (2 Pt 2:4); I am a temple of the Holy Spirit (1 Cor 3:16); I am a member of the Body of Christ; (1 Cor 12:27); I am a citizen of heaven

(Phil 3:20).

- This day I am not my own; I have been bought at a price; I belong to God (1 Cor 6:19-20).
- This day I have died with Christ and sin no longer has power over me (Rom 6:1-6) and the debt against me has been canceled (Col 1:14).
- This day I have been blessed with every spiritual blessing in Christ (Eph 1:3);I can do all things through Christ, who strengthens me (Phil 4:13); I am more than a conqueror (Rom 8:37);
- I have been given the mind of Christ (1 Cor 2:16); I have been firmly rooted in Christ and now being built in him (Col 2:7).
- This day I am God's workmanship (Eph 2:10), I am a minister of reconciliation (2 Cor 5:18).
- This day I am part of a royal priesthood, I am part of a holy nation, I am part of a people set apart to sing God's praises (1 Pt 2:9).
- This day I can come boldly before the throne of God to find mercy and grace in time of need (Heb 4:16).
- This day I will run as if to win (1 Cor 9:24).
- For this is the day the Lord has made. I will rejoice and be glad in it (Ps 118:24).

Daily Prayer for Inner Healing

(Make the Sign of the Cross at this symbol: +)

+Gracious Father, this is the day that you have made for me and I rejoice and am glad in it. +Lord Jesus, this day I accept every blessing that you wish to pour out on my life. +Holy Spirit, I surrender to you and give you permission to conform me in every way to your image and likeness.

Gentle Jesus, meek and humble of heart, Healer of my Soul, and Lover of all mankind, search my memory and make me well. I trust you with all my life, both past, present and future, and determine that nothing of my life be hidden from you. Where I have been wounded, hurt, offended or damaged, pour in the healing Salve of your Mercy, your Holy Spirit. Flood all dark and negative emotions with the Beauty of your Light. Fill my heart with love, joy, peace, patience, kindness, goodness, faithfulness, gentleness, and self-control. You alone are Lord of Time. Do not let the life-lessening events of my past have any power over my present or future. Risen Savior, Conqueror of Death and Vanquisher of Hell, break my chains and set me free!

Just Judge who bears the Wounds of Compassion, it is my will and desire that all who have wounded, hurt, offended or damaged me be forgiven. I cancel all debts I have against them. I choose to forgive and it

165

is my will never to exercise vengeance or punishment upon them. Holy Spirit, stir in their hearts the gift of repentance. Generous Benefactor of Mercy, grant me the grace to forgive from my heart.

I live in the grace of this moment, a moment of healing and freedom through Christ our Lord. AMEN

Life Review Prayer of Forgiveness

Father, you who are rich in mercy, slow to anger, and abounding in compassion, I, your child, born again through the waters of Baptism, filled with the Holy Spirit, thus becoming an inheritor of all the blessings of Christ Jesus, humbly come before you acknowledging that I have sinned. Yet, you, in your loving kindness, have sought to forgive me and welcome me back to the blessings of your kingdom. Since I have been so immeasurably forgiven, I now come to forgive those who have injured, hurt, offended, upset, wronged, ill-treated, slighted, insulted, battered, harmed, or abused me, knowingly or unknowingly, rightly or wrongly. As an act of my free will that you have given me, I choose to forgive and cancel any debt that might be held against this person or these persons. I pray that this prayer would not only come from my thoughts and words, but settle more deeply into my soul and come from my heart.

I depend on your grace, for I am too weak to do this great work of your Gospel on my own. I surrender to the movement of your Holy Spirit upon my life so that he might conform me into the image of your Son, Jesus Christ. Holy Spirit, search my heart and know my inmost being, from the moment of my conception in my mother's womb when you knit me together until this time. Let every relationship lie open before you.

I bring to you every memory and moment with my **parents**. I forgive them for any way they brought pain into my life, purposely or not, rightly or wrongly. I forgive them. I forgive them for any destructive patterns that they passed on to me, whether they be of their own making or passed down through the generations. I proclaim that these patterns no longer have a hold on my life.

Before you, I present the other members of my **family**: my brothers, sisters, grandparents, aunts, uncles, and cousins. You know each of them, Lord, for you have called them by name. To each one I extend a hand of mercy, choosing to forgive. The pain and suffering that I have experienced from them, I do not want them to experience in retaliation. I pray blessings upon them and choose to do good to them in every meeting we will have from this moment on.

Lord, I have been blessed with a great number of **friends** throughout my life. In our daily sharing of life there have been times that I have been offended and have felt rejected by them. It is all these playmates, boyfriend, girlfriend, and comrades, to whom I now hold out a hand of forgiveness. Wherever their lives have taken them, may it be to a place where they are walking with peace in their hearts.

You have destined for man to labor with **fellow employees**. In this work, there have been moments of misunderstanding and competition. It is these whom I now forgive and cancel any debt that I feel or believe they owe me for their behavior that has been unkind, callous or harsh.

In government, there are always those of **authority** placed over us, be it in Church, school, work, or in the government. I bring the memory of these now before your throne of grace. It is my will to revoke any right I have to bring judgment upon them for their actions, teachings, or leadership. May they be blessed with wisdom to continue your work in building a kingdom of justice and equity for all that are under their care.

I remember the ones that are hardest to forgive, **my enemies**. These are the ones Lord, who in full consciousness and enjoyment have set themselves against me. These are the ones who have not been concerned that I have experienced pain, frustration, or anger; or if they have seen my pain, frustration, or anger, they have overlooked it. These have wounded me deep in my soul in a way that cannot be ignored. They have robbed me of life. It has been their will and intent to do me wrong, and therefore, it is now my will and intent to do them well by extending to them my hand and heart, imploring your choicest blessings and graces. I forgive them. May the blessings that are mine be theirs.

Lastly, I bring to you my greatest stumbling block, **myself**. It is I who have sinned against myself, betrayed myself, belittled myself and disappointed myself. Now, I who choose to forgive, cancel, revoke, and write-off any debt that I have against myself. I have been my greatest critic, so I choose, will, and determine to forgive myself.

With the blood of Jesus, by the power of the Holy Spirit, I wash away and now forgive, and will continue to forgive, even on the day of judgment, all offenses that have been committed against me, knowingly or unknowingly, rightly or wrongly. I renounce any stronghold that I have given the enemy due to my anger, annoyance, resentment, bitterness, or apathy.

I accept all the grace with which the Father, the Most High God, would overshadow me, in Jesus' name. AMEN.

Litany of Humility

O Jesus! meek and humble of heart, **Hear me.**

From the desire of being esteemed,
Deliver me, Jesus.
From the desire of being loved...
From the desire of being extolled ...
From the desire of being honored ...
From the desire of being praised ...
From the desire of being preferred to others...
From the desire of being consulted ...
From the desire of being approved ...
From the fear of being humiliated ...
From the fear of being despised...
From the fear of suffering rebukes ...
From the fear of being calumniated ...
From the fear of being forgotten ...
From the fear of being ridiculed ...
From the fear of being wronged ...
From the fear of being suspected ...

That others may be loved more than I,
Jesus, grant me the grace to desire it.
That others may be chosen and I set aside ...
That others may be praised and I unnoticed ...
That others may be preferred to me in everything...
That others may become holier than I, provided that I may become as holy as I should...

Prayer for Deliverance of One's Child
Faith Increasing Principles

Before you enter into prayer, remember these principles.

- God cares for and loves your child more than you can yourself or you can imagine.
- God desires your child's salvation.
- God has a plan for your child's life and is working to bring that plan into force.

Pray a blessing on the person that will lead them into God's plan. God's name is El Kena, The Jealous God. You can trust and you need to trust your child into the hands of God. Here's a great prayer titled *"It Takes what it Takes!"*

> *Father, whatever it takes for my child to come to you and conform to your will, I give you permission and say "yes" to whatever it takes to bring them to this place. In Jesus name. AMEN!*

Most High and Glorious God: Father+, Son+ and Holy Spirit+, I worship and adore you for who you are and all you have given us; and I cry out with all the heavenly host, the Seraphim and the Cherubim, the angels and the Saints: holy, holy, holy, is the Lord, who was, who is, and who is to come.

As I enter into this prayer I repent of any sin and ask for your forgiveness, especially for any sins that (name of child) _____ has committed. *(Here, name the sins your child has committed: unbelief, sexual impurity, drugs and alcohol, self-centeredness, etc. Do not make excuses for their sin. You, also, forgive them for these sins.)*

Holy Trinity, I ask you to cover us, and especially _____, with the blood of the Lamb that has been shed to protect us from the destroying angel.

As _____'s parent, I choose for our family the Lordship of Jesus Christ and bend our knees to Jesus Christ. As _____'s parent it is my choice that our household serves you and you alone. Give our family, and especially _____, all the graces we need to live your abundant life, to be holy, as you, Lord God, are holy.

As I enter into this time of prayer I invite and ask the intercession of the great Mother of God, Mary, most holy, and of all the angels and saints. Father, I invite the ministry of any saint you have assigned for this cause and we thank you for your fatherly care *(Allow the Holy Spirit to bring the name of saints that have been assigned to your need)*. I invite the intercession of _____'s guardian angel, patron saints and name saints.

As _____'s parent, in the name of Jesus, I accept and exercise my God-given authority over _____'s physical, emotional life and spiritual life.

Holy Spirit, please remove all that blocks _____ from receiving and sharing your love and grace. Father, heal any painful wounds in _____'s heart. Heal all genetic, inter-generational, addictive and compulsive concerns and any negative emotions that are conscious or subconscious, known or unknown, against _____ and our family. I also ask that you break all curses that have been cast against our family, in the present or past generations. In Jesus' name, as _____'s parent, I specifically take authority over and break the curses of _____. *(Here, ask the Holy Spirit to show you what your child is truly facing. Then, bring that to prayer. Especially ask to be shown the root of the problems your child is manifesting. Examples: unbelief, depression, anger, unforgiveness, suicide, sexual perversion, drugs, etc. Write those things down).*

Holy Spirit, help _____ to forgive anyone who has hurt him/her, especially any hurt, consciously or unconsciously, rightly or wrongly. I ask that his/her whole person: body and mind, heart and will, soul and spirit, memories and emotions, attitudes and values, fantasies, daydreams, imagination and subconscious be cleansed, renewed and empowered by you, Holy Spirit, and give _____ the grace of hope and joy, the grace to embrace your loving plan for his/her life. *(Ask the Holy Spirit to show you the grace that your child needs in his/her life. Examples: faith, forgiveness, repentance, honesty, peace, etc. Write those things down.)*

In the name of the Father+, Son+ and Holy Spirit+, I, _____'s parent, exercise the authority that is mine over him/her. In Jesus' name, I bind and break any demonic or ungodly influences of friends. In the name of Jesus, as _____'s parent, I render any demonic or ungodly spirits' orders null and void, leaving no area where any negative forces can influence or harm _____. As _____'s parent, I command all these spirits, through the intercession of Mary, the great Mother of God, in the Name of the Father+, the Son+ and the Holy Spirit+, to leave _____ peacefully and quietly and go immediately and directly to the Eucharistic presence of Jesus Christ in the nearest tabernacle to bend their knee to the name of Jesus and be disposed of by Jesus Christ, who is King of Kings and Lord of Lords. In Jesus' name, I command that these spirits never return to harm _____, our family, our circle of friends or anyone else ever again. Father, I ask that you set a hedge of angels to protect us. I command, in Jesus' name, that as these spirits leave, they are bound from any communication with any other spirits. Holy Spirit, please heal and restore the effects of these spirits in and around _____ and any effect they may have had on our family. *(Here, mention any effect that has been had on your family by your child's rebelliousness and pray for restoration. Again, you may need to forgive your child.)*

Holy Spirit, please overshadow _____ as on the day of his/her baptism and flow out from him/her, as Living Water.

Father, increase his/her faith, strengthen his/her hope and deepen his/her love; grant him/her fear of the Lord, piety, counsel, wisdom, fortitude, knowledge and understanding.

170

_____, I, your father/mother, bless you with the desire to seek the Father's holy will and do whatever it takes to fulfill that will.

_____, I, your father/mother, bless you with a desire to draw near to the Sacraments of God's holy Church and I pray all the graces that you have received from the Sacraments in the past come upon you and overtake you now. _____, I bless you with a hunger and a thirst for Christ's Body and Blood in the Eucharist and in the name of Jesus, I call you to receive the Sacraments you need.

Father, I repent of any way that I might have hindered my child from walking in your grace and I ask you to fill any empty places of my parenting with your mercy.

Holy Spirit, place on _____ the Armor of God: the helmet of salvation, the breastplate of righteousness, the belt of truth and shoes of eagerness to spread the good news. Give _____ the sword of the Spirit, which is the Word of God, and the shield of faith to extinguish any fiery darts of the enemy.

Jesus, set _____ totally on fire with your all-consuming and purifying love so _____ can be your light and blessing in the world.

Father, I thank you for the difference that I am going to witness and the blessings we are going to receive because of this prayer, as I pray all this in Jesus' name. Amen!

Daily Prayer for the Poor Souls

SUNDAY
Lord God, by the Precious Blood which Your divine Son, Jesus, shed in the garden, deliver the souls in Purgatory, especially those souls who are the most forsaken of all. Bring them into Your glory where they may praise and bless You forever. Amen. Our Father . . . Hail Mary . . . Eternal rest grant unto them, O Lord. And let perpetual light shine upon them. May they rest in peace. Amen. May their souls and the souls of all the faithful departed, through the mercy of God, rest in peace. Amen

MONDAY
Lord God, by the Precious Blood which your divine Son, Jesus, shed in His cruel scourging, deliver the souls in Purgatory and among them those souls who are nearest to sharing Your glory that they may fully praise and bless You forever. Amen. Our Father . . . Hail Mary . . . Eternal rest grant unto them, O Lord...

TUESDAY

Lord God, by the Precious Blood of Your Divine Son, Jesus, which was shed in His bitter crowning with thorns, deliver the souls in Purgatory, and among them those souls who are in greatest need of our prayers, in order that they may not long be delayed in praising You fully in Your glory and blessing You forever. Amen. Our Father . . . Hail Mary . . . Eternal rest grant unto them, O Lord...

WEDNESDAY

Lord God, by the Precious Blood of Your Divine Son, Jesus, which was shed in the streets of Jerusalem while He carried the Cross, deliver the souls in Purgatory, especially those who are richest in merits in Your sight, so that when they have attained the high place to which they are destined, they may praise You triumphantly and bless You forever. Amen. Our Father . . . Hail Mary . . . Eternal rest grant unto them, O Lord...

THURSDAY

Lord God, by the Precious Body and Blood of Your Divine Son, Jesus, which on the night before His passion He gave to His Beloved Apostles and willed to His Holy Church as a perpetual sacrifice and spiritual nourishment, deliver the souls in Purgatory. Most of all deliver those who were devoted to the mystery of the Eucharist, that they may praise You together with Your Divine Son and the Holy Spirit in Your glory forever. Amen. Our Father . . . Hail Mary . . . Eternal rest grant unto them, O Lord...

FRIDAY

Lord God, by the Precious Blood which Jesus, Your divine Son, shed upon the Cross this day, deliver the souls in Purgatory particularly those souls nearest to me and for whom I should pray, that they may come quickly into Your glory to praise and bless You forever. Amen. Our Father . . . Hail Mary . . . Eternal rest grant unto them, O Lord...

SATURDAY

Lord God, by the Precious Blood which came forth from the sacred side of Your divine Son, Jesus, in the presence and to the great sorrow of His holy Mother, deliver the souls in Purgatory, especially those souls most devoted to this noble Lady, that they may come quickly into Your glory, to praise You with her forever. Amen. Our Father . . . Hail Mary . . . Eternal rest grant unto them, O Lord...

More books from City of the Lord

Manual of Praise
Brendan Case
http://cityofthelord.org/store
Kindle Version $.99
Paper Back $6.95

Do you ever find yourself not knowing what to say when you want to give praise to God?

Do you find yourself saying the same phrases over and over during your time of worship and would like to expand your "praise vocabulary?"

Written by Brendan Case, a dynamic Catholic preacher and worship leader who moves in the prophetic and healing. Brendan encountered the Lord Jesus when he was 16 years old and received the Baptism of the Holy Spirit. For 35 years he has been a leader in the Catholic Charismatic Renewal teaching and inviting believers to the Baptism of the Holy Spirit and a spiritual life based in praise and thanksgiving.

Use this Charismatic Prayer Book to flip back and forth through the pages to find phrases and prayers that will help you enter more fully into your time of worship either by yourself or when you are at a Prayer Meeting.

Tools included are:
Praise Phrases
The Titles of God *(with Bible verses)*
The Hebrew Names of God *(with Bible verses)*
The Names of the Father *(with Bible verses)*
The Names of the Son *(with Bible verses)*
The Names of the Holy Spirit *(with Bible verses)*
Adjectives for Praising
Psalms of Praise and Thanksgiving
Litanies and Akathist of Praise
Prayers of Praise

Keeping Holy the Lord's Day

Gabriel Meyer

http://cityofthelord.org/store

Kindle Version $5.99

Paper Back $8.99

To all who seek to be faithful to God.

As God commanded the Israelites when He gave His Commandments to Moses, "Remember to keep holy the Sabbath." Both Jews and Christians have learned the wisdom of being faithful to this command in the context of the culture in which we live today.

While far too many Christians proclaim they are "too busy" to worship God each Sunday, there are other sincere people of faith who struggle to understand this Commandment beyond the simple obligation to attend Mass.

In his book *Keeping Holy the Lord's Day* Gabriel Meyer provides a profound reflection on the meaning of this Commandment and how a person's life and that of family and community will be enriched if people rediscover and recommit themselves to keeping the Lord's Day holy. While Mr. Meyer presents this material in a manner that is especially suitable for reflection by Catholics. Any person of faith will benefit from reading this work and thinking about how the principles that are expressed can find suitable application in their lives.

Rather than being overcome by the pressures of our contemporary culture with its pressing demands, I commend this book to your reading and trust that you will find it both helpful and challenging as you seek to be faithful to God's command to "keep holy the Sabbath."

Living the Gospel as a Way of Life
James R. Jones
With Gabriel Meyer
Gabriel Meyer
http://cityofthelord.org/store
Kindle Version $8.99
Paper Back $10.99

Today's secular media tends to label Catholic culture as a throwback, an anachronism in the modern world, out of step and out of touch. Whether you are single or married, with children or without, consecrated or laity, new to the faith or a long-time parishioner, *Living the Gospel as a Way of Life* will show you how building a Catholic culture is both possible and relevant for today. This marvelous, timely book provides practical wisdom for those who yearn to build or rebuild a Catholic, Christian culture in their homes, religious orders, or parishes.

Living the Gospel as a Way of Life leads one to reflect seriously on the very personal call to live as a disciple of Jesus and to do so within a relationship with others. At the heart of this book is the positive challenge to live the Gospel as a way of life. We are called to reflect on the question, what is the proper orientation of a person's life if we are focused rightly on loving God first, by living in relationship with others? While honestly facing the truth that life takes a toll on all of us, when we have learned in a positive way to live a "repentant life," we walk in the footsteps of Moses, the Prophets, John the Baptist and Jesus Christ. In this book, you will find helpful principles for developing a spiritual culture in your home and wherever you find yourself, whether with one person or within the context of community life

Made in USA - North Chelmsford, MA
93463_9780991532735
03.23.2024.1327